KENT

KENT

One Hundred Years

Written and edited by
Joan M. Beattie, B.A., M.A., M.Litt.

KENT SCHOOL • KENT, CONNECTICUT 06757

Remember still thy dawn at Kent,
'Till Dawn and darkness are no more.
—Robert S. Hillyer '13

Kent: One Hundred Years
Copyright © 2007 The Kent School

Printed in Canada.

10 9 8 7 6 5 4 3 2 1

International Standard Book Number:
    ISBN 10: 0-9779603-5-8 (Cloth)
    ISBN 13: 978-0-9779603-5-4 (Cloth)
    ISBN 10: 0-9779603-6-6 (Paper)
    ISBN 13: 978-0-9779603-6-1 (Paper)

Produced by:
Moonlight Publishing LLC
2528 Lexington Street
Lafayette, CO 80026 USA
www.moonlight-publishing.com

CONTENTS

Preface

This book is a labor of love. Joan M. Beattie, English Department Chair and holder of the William B. Borsdorff '35 Teaching Chair in English, has presented us with a wonderful chronicle of the School she loves. Her work—*Kent: One Hundred Years*—in turn reflects the contributions in word and deed of countless others who have loved this School and brought it to the beginning of our second century. On the occasion of Kent's Centennial, the entire community is filled with pride in our past and hope for our future.

From its origins in a farmhouse to the modern campus along the Housatonic River that we enjoy today, these chapters tell the remarkable story of Father Frederick Herbert Sill's vision for his Kent School—founded in 1906 on the principles of Simplicity of Life, Directness of Purpose and Self Reliance. For many in the Kent family through the decades, Father Sill was, in the words of the *Reader's Digest*, "my most unforgettable character."

Kent: One Hundred Years profiles some of the many faculty who have given unstintingly of their time and talent to teaching and coaching; some of the many alumni and alumnae who have made lasting contributions to our country and the international community, the arts and professions, business, education, church, and society; and some of the many alumni and parents who have given of their skill and substance to make the dream of a Kent education an enduring one for generations to come.

At the Centennial we salute especially *all* Kent alumni and alumnae—the thousands of graduates who, by their life's work and contributions to their beloved School, have made Kent one of the great schools in the nation.

Today the Kent faculty is as capable and dedicated as any group of teachers preparing young people for college and careers and for lives of service to humanity.

Today Kent provides as much in terms of scholarship assistance to deserving young people, relative to the School's total resources, as any school in America.

Kent is simply a remarkable school: born in austerity; grown by faith; and made permanent by the lifelong commitment of its alumni, faculty, staff, and parents.

To God, who is Love, we give thanks for Kent's one hundred years and for all the families here and abroad who together make up the Kent Family.

—Richardson W. Schell '69
Headmaster & Rector

Acknowledgements

Without the material provided by the following people, this book might never have been written:

The writers and editors of the *Kent News*, beginning in October 1914 and continuing to the present; William Worthington '24; Maitland Edey '28; O. B. Davis '42; Michael West '62; Marcia Kline Sharp '63; Pim Goodbody '55; Brandon Sweitzer '60; Mark McWhinney '75; Daniel Perkins '93; Andrew Schneider '00; Kent Alley '82; Michael Graae '07; Curtis Scofield. I am especially grateful to Thomas Holcombe for his histories of St. Joseph's Chapel and the organ. Kathy Nadire, Liesel Krueger, and Marc Cloutier were of great help in providing information and scanning photographs. Numerous other people sent reminiscences, some of which have found their way in part into the text and some of which will appear, or have appeared, in the *Kent Quarterly* in some form during the centennial year and the year following. My gratitude to all of these contributors is enormous.

I want to thank publisher Rick Rinehart '72 for his guidance, encouragement, and patience throughout the process of creating this book.

Marel d'Orbessan Rogers '65 receives my special thanks and appreciation for her encouragement and help as supplier and scanner of pictures and reader of the text as it evolved.

Special thanks, too, to Elaine Griffin who provided moral support throughout the project – which seemed unending at times.

And finally, to the headmaster, Richardson W. Schell, my very special thanks for trusting me with the writing of this book and for his unwavering encouragement and enthusiastic support.

—Joan M. Beattie

Photo by Frank Celenza

An Ode

To Celebrate the Fiftieth Anniversary
of the Founding of Kent School

So imperceptibly the seasons went
That, like a man who stops to catch his breath
Climbing a hill, not knowing the extent,
Until he turns, of vistas spread beneath,
Now looking back on fifty years of Kent
That seem miraculous rewards of faith
We see, for the first time, the entire range
Of things achieved and things that do not change.

A young man's dream is what Kent started from –
And so may it remain until the end!
The man who was to be in years to come
Pater to many hundreds, priest and friend,
Came to this place and chose it as our home,
Blest acreage where hills and harvest blend,
Set between creek and river on this meadow
Like a great sundial for Mount Algo's shadow.

The Pater, in my memory appearing
As prophet of a schoolboy's joy or doom,
Teaching and overseeing, loudly cheering
The team, or quelling the Assembly room,
Was like the weather, clouding and then clearing:
A climate to bring hardy youth to bloom.
I see him finally in a golden mist
Of candlelight, singing the Eucharist.

By grace of God, the Pater lived to share
With hundreds what he once had dreamed alone.
In his white habit he was everywhere
As wooden walls gave way to brick and stone
Until, in those last years, an invalid's chair
Became him like a patriarchal throne.
Another priest and friend now fires at Kent
New zeal in the benign experiment.

(continued)

And, after many years, on my return,
Half fearful, as alumni are, of change,
I find a nobler school where I discern
The inspiring guidance in a wider range
Of this headmaster's guardianship, and learn
How things may grow without becoming strange,
The new proceeding from the old recast,
Rich, but not overburdened, with the past.

Three wars have taken toll of us, and peace,
Too like a war suspended for a time,
Has, through anxiety without surcease,
Taken as many others in their prime.
These are our saints and heroes; their release
 Binds us to nobler effort. Every chime
 That rings out from our Chapel is, for them,
 Among the echoing hills, a requiem.

Their names are cast for ever in the heart
More lasting than bronze monument; we deem
Them fortunate as time goes on; apart
From mortal change and destiny, they seem
One with life's early rising, with the start
Of joy unshadowed by its end, the dream
Of youth transmuted to reality,
And all their past a glory still to be.

So many of them who were friends remain
As last I knew them, the undying young;
One with my studies, the clear Classic strain
Of beauty's symmetry, the songs unsung
Made perfect in their silence; and again
I walk with boyhood through the woods among
Unfading flowers and up the shining river
Whose moods and music haunt my blood for ever.

In winter nights I lay awake and heard
The black ice booming in the ruthless cold.
Then, as the warmer weather came, it stirred
And broke and, in a mad upheaval, rolled
Downstream, uprooting trees and, uncontrolled
By banks, half took them with it. Days on end
The loud-voiced water brawled around the bend.

Advancing spring, pervasive and serene,
Assuaged the river that with calmer powers
Resumed its hemlock-shadowed flow between
The banks now covered over with wild flowers;
While on its surface, smooth as a machine,
The first shell cut the water, and the rowers
With unphrased happiness at spring returning
Strained to the rythmic pull, their long oars churning.

Compared to present days the school was poor,
But the essential spirit was the same;
The nucleus of virtues that endure
Foretold what affluently Kent became:
The Library, the shrine of literature,
The Chapel, shrine of sacramental flame,
Were scarcely more than sheds, but faith and learning
Though humbly housed were no less brightly burning.

Blest was the school where so much brightness shone
From frugal windows in that simple place.
Blest is the school that grows as Kent has grown
Without diminishment of zeal or grace.
Truth does not weaken when more widely sown,
Nor vision become dim in ampler space;
For every hill we climb, a higher hill
Reveals unfolding vistas further still.

In this wide valley where we learned to live,
Hailing the past, we face futurity.
Our Numeral Rock of fifty years we give
To Thee, great Architect of time; To Thee
Our thanks and praise that years so fugitive
Are built into Thy hills eternally
To be the starting point for those who climb
The paths of light beyond the cliffs of time.

—Robert Silliman Hillyer '13

The titles of the five main sections of this history are taken from this ode.

I
A Young Man's Dream
Father Sill and the First Years at Kent

In 1906, Kent, Connecticut, was a small rural community, surrounded by hills, defined in part by the Housatonic River that flowed along the town's western edge, a stop on the New York, New Haven, and Hartford railroad as it journeyed toward Montreal. About twelve hundred people called Kent home, and most of them had probably never been very far from that home with the exception of those who had fought in the two major wars, the Revolution and the Civil War, men remembered on the monument that stood where the dirt road from the south and the dirt road running east and west met.

That year a young priest with a vision came to Kent to found his school, a school where young men of slender means could gain an education second to none. What brought him to the valley? At first, chance — or perhaps he would have said God — and the river, of course, for he was an oarsman, coxswain of the Columbia crew, and the river with its promise of crew must have been one of the things that drew The Reverend Frederick Herbert Sill to Kent.

Who was this young man with a dream? Frederick Herbert Sill was born in New York City on March 10, 1874. He was a graduate of Columbia University (1894) and the General Theological Seminary, a monk of the Order of the Holy Cross, a visionary, a man of faith, and a consummate businessman. The son of an Episcopal priest, he saw the need for a Church School for boys whose parents could not afford the expense of the existing boarding schools.

A tribute to Father Sill from the Class of 1941 on the occasion of their sixtieth reunion in 2001 perhaps helps to tell the story.

> When we [the Class of 1941] arrived at Kent School as twelve-year-old Second Formers in the fall of 1936, members of the Class of 1941 were terrified at their first encounter with "The Great White Tent" — the Reverend Frederick Herbert Sill, O.H.C., Headmaster and Founder of Kent School. Smoking his curved pipe and wearing his yellowing monastic robes, he had the appearance of great antiquity. He fiddled constantly with the dials on his hearing aid, making two-way conversation difficult. Father Sill was unlike anything most of us had ever seen

Right: The Order of the Holy Cross at West Park, New York.

before. Yet he was kindly in his welcome, and during visits to his attic study in the old Main Building, we came to realize that he cared about each one of us, and that he was keenly committed to develop in us the values, self-discipline, and responsibility expressed in the school's motto.

Where did such a man come from? What shaped his decision to found a school based on sound moral principles, and develop generations of young leaders? Here are a few glimpses of Frederick Sill as a young man, and of a few of the influences that produced this pioneering educator.

The principal influence on Father Sill's development was undoubtedly his father, The Reverend Thomas H. Sill, an Episcopal minister, who, following the Civil War, accepted the challenge of establishing a Mission for Trinity Church to serve the poor in the "Tenderloin" district of New York City. He continued to operate his mission chapel, always interested in children, serving for forty-five years as chaplain of the children's hospital, and as warden for a home for crippled children. He was concerned about social conditions and worked hard for improving the lot of working people. An eyewitness description of mourners at his funeral in 1910 conveys his impact on the people of his community:

"The night before the funeral, as the body lay in St. Chrysostom's Chapel and mourners came to take a farewell look at the face of him they loved so well, it was a study to note the classes represented. Now a man of wealth and standing in his community, following him a poor woman, then a stalwart policeman in his uniform, after him a letter carrier, then one of the young men of the choir, and so it went on, through the night."

Thomas Sill's son, Frederick, was only thirty-two years old in 1906 when he founded Kent School. Adopting a revolutionary premise of sliding scale tuitions, Father Sill changed boarding school education from a refuge for the children of the wealthy, to a training ground for future leaders in a democratic society. We were the last class to graduate under his headmastership, after thirty-five years of service, and count ourselves very lucky to have come under his gruff but benign influence.

While conducting a mission in St. Louis with Fr. James O. S. Huntington, the Superior of the Order of the Holy Cross, Father Sill was given permission to start organizing the school he envisioned. In March 1906, a booklet was issued stating the need for funds to start a school "to provide at a minimum cost for boys of ability and character, who must presumably upon graduation be self-supporting, a combined academic and commercial course of instruction, and also preparation for college and university courses. Simplicity of life, self-reliance, and directness of purpose are to be especially encouraged in the boys." Seven New York men formed a Committee on Organization and Incorporation: A.G. Paine Jr., Chairman; Frederic P. Keppel; Albert W. Putnam; John A. Dix; Howard Sherwood; C.E. Kneeland; and R. S. Pierrepont; with Father Sill serving as Secretary of the Committee. Money was raised to get things underway, and on a serendipitous visit to Kent, a building was rented. Later, when the School was incorporated these men served as the first Board of Trustees. In addition a Council of Seven was named, consisting of the Reverend Endicott Peabody, D.D.; the Reverend W. G. Thayer, D.D.; the Reverend W. T. Manning, S.T.D.; the Reverend J.O.S. Huntington, O.H.C.; Colonel E.A. Stevens; Mr. John W. Wood; and Mr. Guy Richards.

* * * * *

Father Sill first saw Kent when he came down from Pittsfield on the train to bring communion to Mrs. Howard Thayer, a friend of Fr. Huntington's. Howard Thayer drove Father Sill along the Housatonic, down to Bull's Bridge, and then up the west side of the river where they saw the old Fuller farmhouse, the residence of Clarence Fuller. Both men saw it as a promising location for a school, even though the house was in bad condition and had no indoor plumbing. As Father Sill reminisced about those early days, he recalled that that problem was easily remedied by the town plumber, Gene Bull, who was also the Board of Health, coroner, and undertaker. Chance had brought Father Sill to the west bank of the Housatonic, and, later that year, it brought him

*Above: The memorial window in
St. Joseph's Chapel for Father Huntington,
founder of the Order of the Holy Cross.*

Statement of finances April 22. 1906

Total received from all sources   8242.20

" expended for Pyst 1 = May 1   6423.93

                          Bal. on hand   1818.27

To carry school to July 1.   1310.00

                                  Bal.   508.27

Still due from fees.   555.00

"   "   "   gifts   1340.00

                                        # 2403.27

Pledged on acc. 1907-8.   + 1936.00

a bit further north to the present site of the school, the Jeremiah Fuller farm. The story of the first year of Kent School, 1906-1907, has entered the realm of myth and legend, but it is worth recounting, at least in part, one more time. In a talk during a Corporate Communion of the School on the Feast of St. Michael and All Angels marking the 30th anniversary of the founding of the School, Father Sill described his arrival in Kent and the early days of the School. "I got off the train at the railway station in town and Mr. Thayer was there waiting for me with a horse and buggy. The horse was a bob-tailed old mare with about five hairs in her tail. Mr. Thayer drove me over to his house at the other side of the town where he put me up for the night.

"By the time I had celebrated Holy Communion the next morning I was too late to catch the train back to Pittsfield, so Mr. Thayer suggested that we take a little drive down the other side of the river. We drove in the same horse and buggy down that sandy, dusty road to Bull's Bridge. All the way down we talked over my plans for the school. I told him at the time that I was having trouble finding a situation for it. . . . On the way back we stopped in at the old Indian Reservation and I paid my respects to the Indian Princess buried there.

"Up the river a little way from the [Indian] reservation was Clarence Fuller's old place, an old run-down farmhouse. We got out and inspected the

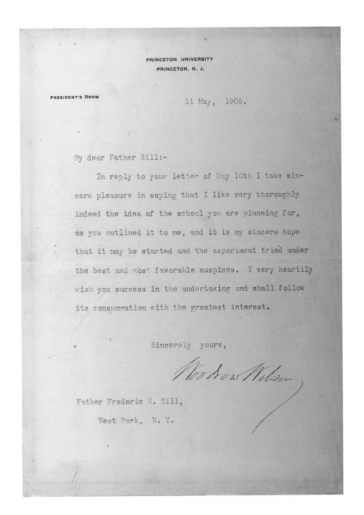

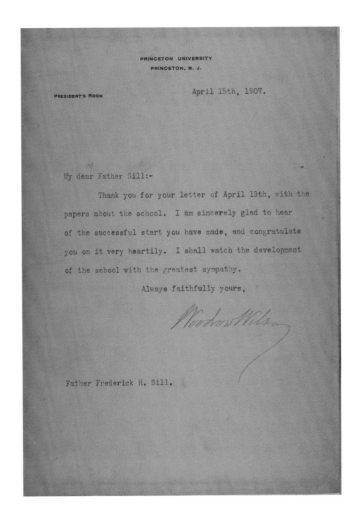

Above: *Two letters from Woodrow Wilson when he was president of Princeton.*

building, and before we left, I had rented it for $40 a month. In order to assure Mr. Fuller that I was in earnest I left him a ten dollar deposit. That accounts for the situation of the school" (*The Kent News*, October 7, 1936).

After cleaning up the place and having a bathroom installed (one of the few in the town), ordering beds (which didn't arrive in time for the opening of school), and getting in food, (Father Sill said, "I think that I ordered enough Shredded Wheat for the whole School for the entire year. The canned baked beans lasted two years."), all was ready for the first scholars and their three masters. The first student to arrive was Anson Gardner.

"It was not a particularly auspicious arrival, the station being dark when the evening train reached Kent. No one was at the station but the stationmaster, no conveyance of any kind and no signs of any place to spend the night. We learned that two maiden ladies, the Hopsons I believe, sometimes took in guests, so we walked up the street and found they were willing to take us in for the night. . . .

"I shall never forget my dismay when arriving at the site of the school the next morning. There seemed to be absolutely no signs of anything other than a typical old farm rather run down at the heel. . . . I don't remember just how it happened that I arrived before the other boys, but it was fortunate that

Right: The Charter Masters and Scholars.

we straggled in one or two at a time as we were able to get things more or less shipshape by the day of the great opening" (Anson Gardner, *The Kent News*, November 20, 1935).

    And open the School did, with three masters – Lloyd Holsapple (who was delayed by the death of his father), Eben Haley, and Theodore Hobbie— and some eighteen to twenty boys: Arthur Lacey Baker, Andrew Bedford Galatian, Anson B. Gardner, James White Harriss, Edward Ridgeley Harrison, John Cameron Hawkins, Walter Charles Hottes, Edgar R. Jackman Jr., Clifford H. Lane, James P. Boniface Langford, Donald Stuart McNulty, Osgood Perry, Reginald Dwight Perry, Edward Connor Stradley, Alfred H. Sweet, Leonard Graeme Taylor, Herbert Francis Thorpe, Elliott W. Underhill, and Cuthbert Vail Wright. As a matter of record, the photograph of the charter masters and scholars reproduced here and in *Fifty Years: 1906-1956 Kent School* identifies all of these young men and their three masters. However, in *The Kent Year Book* of 1913 Wade H. Thompson is also named as a Charter Scholar.

    According to all accounts, the first night was memorable. Father Sill had engaged a family of four, a husband and wife and their daughter and son, to cook and serve. The father "found friends of the wrong type and was continually in a condition that was hardly satisfactory. . . . the daughter was afflicted with tuberculosis. That left the mother to cook, and her son to wait on table." However, the cook took ill before the end of the evening meal, so that the corn cakes that were on the menu had not been baked although the cook had prepared the batter. Father Sill, ever the optimist, felt sure that he could bake something so simple; "one would think anyone could. Well, I don't know whether it was my fault or the fault of the batter, but by the time the cakes were wholly done, they were just as hard as this table. The floor of the dining-room had just been waxed, and as the waiter entered, he slipped and made a perfect three-point landing. The corn cakes went bouncing in all directions, but as I knew the floor was clean, I collected the cakes and put them back on the plate. The waiter was so embarrassed that he refused to do any more waiting," so the boys all pitched in and waited on their guests and themselves. That, said Father Sill, "was really the birth of the self-help system."

After sending the boys to bed early, Father Sill and Masters Haley and Hobbie sat down to make out a schedule of studies. "I heard a noise upstairs. Just as I was about to leave to settle things the whole crowd of 18 appeared at the doorway of the room in bathrobes and all sorts of adornments. They had come down to tell us, as they did through Cameron Hawkins, that they would back us up in anything we did for their welfare. They managed to give the Kent cheer K-K-K-K, E-E-E-E, N-N-N-N, T-T-T-T, KENT! This was a good sign. I had taught them the cheer during the day. It was the first time they had given the cheer and it sounded mighty well" (*Kent Quarterly* Winter 1983, reprinted from the *Kent News* article in the fall of 1944).

The next day, the Feast of St. Michael and All Angels, September 29, 1906, the first Eucharist was celebrated at Kent School. "That afternoon we had a public reception to which the whole town of Kent was asked. It was quite a problem to handle all those people [some fifty people appeared] and to find places to hitch the horses. There was a big flag in front of the building. Tea was served. Mr. John Hopson gave the official welcome to the School on behalf of the town of Kent" (*The Kent News*, October 7, 1936).

And so the School began its journey, which has reached the century mark. Dinner is no longer creamed codfish and corn cakes, but the Kent cheer can be heard in the Dining Hall on occasion and the self-help system continues to this day, though modified a bit by various state restrictions.

Left: The Feast of St. Michael and All Angels, September 29, 1906. Father Sill invited the whole town of Kent to a reception at which tea was served.

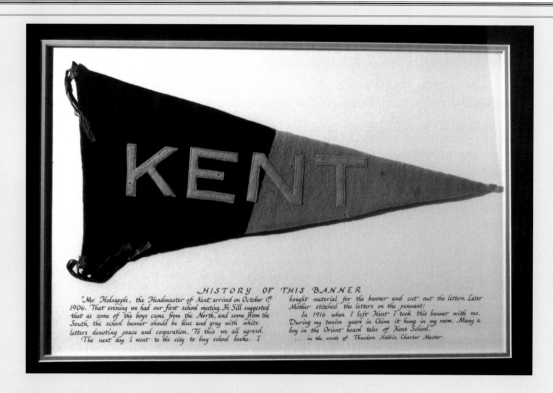

THE ORIGIN OF THE BLUE AND GREY

When the Kent News offered a prize in 1975 to anyone who could tell when, how, and why the School colors became blue and grey, Theodore Hobbie, a Charter Master of the School, replied with an explanation.

Mr. Holsapple, the headmaster of Kent, arrived October 1, 1906. That evening we had our first school meeting. Fr. Sill suggested that as some of the boys came from the North and some from the South, the school flag should be blue and gray with white letters denoting peace and cooperation. To this we all agreed.

The next day I went to the city to buy school books. I also bought material for the flag, cut out the letters, and Mother made the flag.

In 1916 when I left Kent I took this flag with me: and during my twelve years in China it hung in my room. Many a boy in the Orient heard tales of the Kent School.

—Frère Hobbie

In the spring of 1907, Father Sill finally found a permanent site for the School. Again, "by chance," the right place was found, the Jeremiah Fuller house and farm on the west side of the bridge over the Housatonic, near where the Administration Building stands today. Miss Lizzy Fuller wanted to sell her property and, while there were problems and the buildings were in poor condition, the price seemed right: $3000 cash and a $3000 mortgage. While Father Sill did not have $3000 in cash, he had never let that stop him. After all, he had begun his school just months before with a mere $200. He immediately went into town and borrowed $50 from Charles Eaton, a good friend to the

School. Then he returned to Miss Fuller and told her that he would buy the farm. She gave him three weeks to raise the money. He got on the next train to New York City and began raising the money, a task he described as "tough work." The final $1000, enough to put him over the top, came from two friends, Dr. Henry Ferguson, Rector of St. Paul's School, Concord, New Hampshire, and Mrs. Thomas Nickerson, the wife of the rector of St. Stephen's Episcopal Church in Pittsfield, Massachusetts, and the daughter of Dean Hoffman of the General Theological Seminary. Father Sill returned to Kent, repaid Charles Eaton's loan, got the town clerk to make out the deed for the property, and took the check for $3000 to Miss Fuller. Father Sill said, "She belonged to the small group that said the school would fail," so she insisted on waiting until she had the money in cash before she gave him the title to the property and the mortgage papers.

It was then that Father Sill sent out his first general appeal for Kent School. It stated that "'The School was incorporated under the Laws of the State of Connecticut on February 7, 1907, the legal title being the Kent School Corporation.'"

The letter continued:

> A farm has been secured with an old Colonial farmhouse and an ideal site for permanent buildings, with athletic field and facilities for water sports, and within easy walking distance of Kent Village. By resolution of the Board of Trustees, the firm of Grosvenor Atterbury, architects of 20 West 43rd Street, New York City, was selected to prepare plans for whatever improvements were to be made or new buildings erected. A representative from Mr. Atterbury's office has visited the new site and plans have been prepared for remodeling the present house and adding to it a building with dormitories, schoolroom, recitation-rooms, laboratories and gymnasium.
>
> It is estimated that the sum of 25,000 dollars will be required to carry out the proposed plan. This includes furnishing, heating, etc. as well as actual construction. It is hoped that the above amount will be contributed in time to have the work done this summer. The proposed buildings will provide for 32 boys, and five masters, beside those engaged in the household work.

Prize Day that first year was held on the front lawn, facing west. Lloyd Holsapple had served as the first headmaster when Fr. Huntington insisted that Father Sill remain in residence at West Park. By the end of the first year, however, he had relented, and the Trustees had met and elected Father Sill headmaster. No boys graduated that year, but, as Father Sill wrote, "we were all set for the autumn term in our real school."

Right: Kent School in 1907.

Below: The Kent Quarterly,
Vol. I, Numbers 1 and 2.

The Kent Quarterly

VOL. I.   NUMBERS 1 AND 2

SINGLE COPIES TWENTY-FIVE CENTS

Board of Editors for 1908-1909.

C. A. CRAWFORD, '09.   A. B. GARDNER, P. G.
R. P. TITUS, '09.   R. B. HILL, '10.
J. C. HAWKINS, '09.   E. B. BERKELEY, '10.

THE QUARTERLY

In THE QUARTERLY it is the purpose of the Kent School body to publish a chronicle of events, in a word, a news magazine, rather than the ordinary preparatory school publication. The latter is apt to be but a medium for the infliction of puerile schoolroom themes on those who, guided by a generous interest in the school, subscribe to the magazine, though it is doubted if many of these subscribers read any articles save those phenomenal compositions of their own prodigious "hopefuls." It is our purpose, through THE QUARTERLY to keep our friends in touch with our work, our play, our accomplishments, and our aspirations. It is not our purpose to waste the printer's time setting up classroom themes and near-stories. Nothing will appear that is not actively pertinent to Kent School life.

In deciding to publish our magazine four times a year we were guided by the time-honored maxim "Quality rather than quantity." We plan to issue the numbers in the four seasons suggested by All Saints, Christmas, Easter, and Commencement, hoping thus, by not crowding the numbers, to maintain a standard which will make THE QUARTERLY a "worth while" publication. In this first issue we hope to have taken the first step towards setting such a standard.

                                                    C. A. C.

In the fall of 1907 the number of boys had increased to thirty-two, and the first prefects were named: Anson Gardner, Osgood Perry, and Alfred Sweet. There were six forms, first to sixth, with the oldest boys essentially in charge of the younger ones. Mr. Holsapple had resigned in order to study at Oxford, and Mr. Haley taught French and English (or German, according to at least one account), and Mr. Hobbie taught mathematics and science. Father Sill taught Sacred Studies, Latin, Greek, and English. Three new members of the faculty had been appointed; Mr. Gano to teach mythology, history, and Latin; Mr. Whittingham to teach English and history; and Mr. Kibby to teach Greek and Latin.

From the beginning Father Sill had a vision of a permanent Kent, a Kent of fireproof brick buildings that would serve countless generations of schoolboys, but the first Kent was a conglomeration of white clapboard buildings, beginning with Lizzy Fuller's farmhouse, now Old Main. It stood across from the current administration building, facing the river. Later that year, the building was enlarged to include a dining room, kitchen, and laundry. There were pigpens where the dining hall stands today, and a red barn on the site of North Dorm.

On Ascension Day 1908, the first chapel was dedicated, the gift of Miss Estelle Ogden. In the summer of 1909, the main wooden building was erected, and in the summer of 1911 the old barn and infirmary were built, all wooden structures. "Just about five o'clock Sunday evening, November 19, 1911, those who were about the house and immediate neighborhood, were startled by the fire-bell. Any doubt as to whether it was simply a fire-drill was dispelled by the lurid glare of the flames bursting from the Mathematics Class room. . . . At first it seemed as

Left: Kent School in 1911.

though the whole building was doomed. The heroic work of George Baker, the Superintendent of the farm, who went right into the burning rooms with a chemical extinguisher, followed by the prompt action of the well-trained School Fire Brigade with the big hose, the extinguisher and the buckets, held the flames in check" (*Kent Quarterly*, December 1911). Disaster had been averted, at least for the time being.

The original St. Joseph's Chapel was completed in 1913, and the wooden quad in 1914. The sixth form clubhouse, the Form House, was built on the hill where the Rectory built by Father Patterson stands today. Electricity

Left: St. Joseph's Chapel in 1914.

Right: The interior of St. Joseph's Chapel.

Below left: The school in 1914.
Below right: The tennis courts were next to the chapel in 1914.

came to Kent in 1915. Ten years after the first scholars and three masters arrived, in the fall of 1916, Kent had grown to ten masters and 131 students.

Building continued; in 1917 the Old Field House that was near the present Boat House and Rowing Center, in 1918 "Faculty Row" houses north of the Field House. Kent was well established, but it was not yet what Father Sill had envisioned, a permanent Kent.

If Kent were merely buildings, this story would have bones but no flesh, but Kent is more than that. During these years of creating a physical structure, Father Sill was building a place of learning and worship, where young men would be nourished spiritually, physically and intellectually. The boys went to chapel eight times a week, once on Monday through Saturday and twice on Sunday. Each week each boy wrote a letter home, and each week grades were posted. They played football, hockey, and tennis, coached by Father Sill; they worked on the farm—an institution probably unique among the elite prep

Left: The campus from the river in 1915.

schools of the day; they stoked furnaces and cleaned bathrooms; they chopped wood and picked apples.

In October 1914, the *Kent News* appeared for the first time, reporting the opening of school on its front page and news of the athletic contests held the previous week. The issues that followed included the subject of Father Sill's Sunday sermon and sermons given by visiting dignitaries from the Order of the Holy Cross and other ecclesiastical institutions, the boys' grades for the week, news of special events, and advice to new boys. Editorials were written about the school's motto. Concern was voiced about the war. News of the farm told of the "excellent hay crop, more than the barn could hold. The oats were harvested at just the right time. They had fine full heads. The corn also proved a record crop. The potato crop is still to be harvested. In connection with the summer's work it is interesting to note that already over 2000 quart jars of fruit and vegetables have been preserved, most of them coming from the school yield" (*Kent News*, September 27, 1918). That November the *News* reported that forty barrels of apples had been picked, and later that month, the end of the Great War was announced.

But life was not just books and shoveling coal

Below: Kent School News, Vol. 1, No. 1.

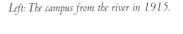

Kent School News

VOL. 1. NO. 1.   SATURDAY, OCTOBER 10, 1914   KENT, CONN.

LOST BY A POINT

Game with Taft Contested Hotly to the End.

On September 26 Kent lost her opening game to Taft School at Watertown. Both teams showed lack of practice, but, on the whole, were well matched, the play tending to favor the Taft team on account of its superior weight and speed. In spite of this disadvantage, the Kent team fought splendidly and proved its worth when, in the last period with only a few minutes to play, it braced and held the Taft eleven on our one foot line. Considering the small amount of practice that the team has had, this exhibition was remarkable.

Were it not for the rather high northerly wind blowing down the Taft field, weather conditions would have been ideal for football.

Shortly after 3 o'clock the game began. Captain Atkins, of Taft, winning the toss, chose to receive at the north goal. Ash kicked off to Kissel who ran the ball back 12 yards. Taft was forced to punt, and Hamilton receiving on Kent's five yard line, was downed without covering any distance. Here Kent was forced to kick out of danger, but Taft after reaching the five yard line again fumbled to Kent. In three plays Kent made first down only to be held by the consistent work of the Taft line and was forced to punt. After two short gains by Hyde and Henger and a ten yard penalty for Taft offside, Prout blocked Henger's kick, but Kent did not manage to get possession of the ball. On the next play, however, Taft fumbled and Cory, with five Kent men for interference, carried the ball 40 yards for a touchdown. Ash failed to kick the goal and immediately after the next kickoff time was called.

The second period opened with the teams in mid-field. Taft made first down working Henger and Spurr, who displaced Hyde, only to have Hamilton neatly intercept a forward pass and cover five yards before being downed. Kent was compelled to punt, the ball dribbling over the back line. After Taft had made first down by long runs of Spurr and Henger, Pierson intercepted another forward pass, getting away for ten yards. But

(Continued on Fourth Page.)

THE OPENING OF SCHOOL.

Work Begins With Enrollment of 120 and 35 New Fellows.

School opened very successfully on Sept. 16, for its ninth year, with an enrollment of 120 boys, 35 of them being new fellows. The regular work was begun the next day, the 17th, and all settled down to the regular term's work.

Although several of the older fellows were absent on account of college examinations, they were all back, with one exception, by Monday, the 21st. These fellows began work immediately, and as they had missed only two or three days of school, were able to make up their work and start with their classes right away.

The candidates for the football team were called out on Thursday, the 17th, for their first practice, and from that time forward were drilled every day in preparation for the opening game at Taft.

Thus far the departments of the school work and sports have been started without delay, and as the fellows set to with a will everything began well, so that it undoubtedly was the most successful opening of the year's work in the history of the school.

CHEERING GREATLY NEEDED.

Football Team Entitled to Backing of the School.

Monday and Tuesday the whole school went down to the stands after dinner to practice cheering. The new fellows have responded heartily; have come off snappy.

The cheering is only fairly good. Perhaps it is because it is early in the season. The team needs all the backing every individual fellow can give.

The cheer leaders for this year are Dehon and Skelding I.

THE MUSICAL CLUB.

The first meeting of the Musical Club was called Sunday, Sept. 27. Of last year's club the following were present: Mr. Shelley, Prout, Wells, Skelding, Whitman and Magruder. The following new boys reported: Du Pont, Boyd, Gallup, Van den Arend, Bass and Schuyler.

Although the absence of many of last year's members will be greatly felt, nevertheless the prospects for the coming year are very good.

PAWLING VICTOR

Kent School Unable to Hold Heavier Eleven.

A fast and exciting game was played with Pawling on the Kent Field last Wednesday, which resulted in a defeat for Kent. It is only right to say, however, that Kent throughout the game was working against a much heavier team, and that taking this into consideration Kent did wonderfully well to hold the visitors down to the 23 to 6 score.

On the line Taft, Prout, Cory and Harris all played a consistent game, while in the backfield Nadal and Hamilton starred. From beginning to end Pawling played good fast football, and showed a marked improvement over last year both in speed and weight and in the way the team was run. The game by quarters was as follows:

FIRST PERIOD.

Winning the toss, Kent chose to kick, Pawling defending the south goal. Ash kicked off to Patterson, who covered ten yards on the run back. Twenty more yards around end by O'Neil netted first down, but Kent took a brace and held Pawling for downs. On the first play Nadal went through tackle for 15 yards. Hamilton added five more, only to have Patterson intercept a forward pass on the next line-up. A penalty for holding forced Captain Patterson to punt out of danger. Then followed some aggressive work on the part of Kent. Nadal was jammed through the line for three yards, and then ran, on a fake forward pass, for ten yards. A two yard gain, coupled with eight yards by Hamilton, netted first down, but Kent was held and the period ended with the ball on Pawling's 20 yard line.

SECOND PERIOD.

Gargan went through the line for eight yards. Pawling was penalized and Patterson punted to Hamilton. An end run by Nadal and a trick pass, Pierson to Hamilton, brought Kent to the 35 yard line. Here Ash attempted a drop kick, but failed by a small margin, the ball hitting the inside of one of the goal posts and bouncing back into the field. Pawling was held on the 35 yard line after two short

(Continued on Fourth Page.)

Above: Kent boys drilling at the Kent railroad station.

on cold winter mornings to keep the furnaces going. While the boys were not allowed to cross the bridge over the Housatonic to enjoy the delights of the town, they did have the "pop" tent where they could spend their allowances, and Saturday night school meetings, which included speeches by students, were a highlight of the weekend. If this sounds fairly tame to 21st century readers, one must remember that in those halcyon days, life was indeed simpler. And there were the School holidays: St. Michael and All Angels, which was also Founder's Day, September 29th, All Saints Day on November 1, the Feast of the Purification on February 2nd, Easter Monday, and Ascension Day. They began with the Eucharist, and many of them included work around the campus. Boys went for walks, played games, and enjoyed a brief respite from classes. Occasionally a work holiday was announced so that the boys could take care of special chores. While the boys did, of course, go home for Christmas, Thanksgiving was celebrated at the School and was a joyful day when families arrived to feast with their sons. And on April 1, 1909, a tradition began when the class of 1910 painted its class numbers in purple and gold on what became know as Numeral Rock.

Kent was not, however, immune to the problems of the larger world, and the boys began drilling in preparation for their being called to military service. Finally, on April 6, 1917, the United States entered the Great War being waged an ocean away. An editorial in the *News* on April 7, 1917, speaking of those who were considering enlisting, said, "Many fellows have already determined to enlist; many more are considering the matter most gravely, and we rejoice at being able to say of these fellows that their action is not a mere flare of impelling adventure, but rather the outcome of a deep-rooted patriotism. We shall be sad at their departure; proud of their loyalty. They shall represent Kent School." Very soon, the *Kent News* began to print the letters faculty and alumni who were fighting in Europe had written to Father Sill.

Printed in the *News* on April 21, 1917, one particularly moving letter came from Edwin Abbey, who had come to Kent in 1909 after leaving the university because he was ill. He was a master for one year, leaving to continue his studies at the University of Pennsylvania. In a letter to Father Sill he wrote that he had enlisted in the 2nd Battalion Canadian Pioneers on October 2, 1915. In a later letter, dated March 11, 1917, he wrote of trench warfare and the cold and mud. "December was soft and toward the end the trenches began to cave in and fill up with mud. January for three weeks was unspeakable. The trenches became absolutely impassible; they were filled with liquid soapy mud, hip-deep and in some places over your head. All movement had to be 'overland' after dark.

In daytime it was a case of man the trenches and stay where you were, with the dubious consolation that Fritz was in the same plight.

"Then it began to freeze up and we had a month of bitter cold, unprecedented in France. The trenches dried up, the walls hardened and everything was cold but rosy. . . .

"This period is about over now and we are expecting to return to mud which will smash all previous records though latterly it has been quite cold again. I am looking forward to my first experience of a big offensive before I am much older. . . .

"I anxiously wait for news of a declaration of war by the United States. It seems inevitable after the Mexican conspiracy and to me the delay seems dangerous. . . .

"Our news is all good, and the army is filled with confidence and determination though the work ahead is difficult and may take a long time. The men are ready to make every sacrifice and have the spirit that means Victory."

By one of those strange coincidences that seem to color all lives, on Easter Monday, April 9, 1917, several weeks before the letter above was printed in the *News*, Father Mayo spoke of Edwin Abbey to the boys, quoting some of his earlier letters. At that time, he was the only person connected with Kent who had actually been in the fighting on the front. "At almost the very hour that Father Mayo was speaking in the School, Lieutenant Abbey was leading a charge of Canadian troops up the slope of Vimy Ridge. The result of the battle that day will be recorded as one of the turning points of the war. In that charge, on that Easter Monday, Edwin Abbey gave his life for what he considered to be the cause of God and humanity. Knowing how he loved Kent School as a result of his connection with the School as a member of the faculty, it is very significant that he should have been recalled and cheered on the very day he was leading his charge" (*Kent School News*, May 12, 1917).

Above: The Edwin Abbey memorial in the John Gray Park Library.

The *Kent News* printed a list of Kent men in the service in September 1918, and in 1936, in a column entitled "Thirty Years at Kent," the *News* reported that "It was indeed under adverse conditions that the thirteenth year began at Kent. With two-thirds of its number absent, these having answered the country's call, it meant that an overwhelming percentage of new boys must absorb Kent's spirit and tone. . . . Among those who left in September to offer their services in the event of the War was Dixon Walker, a prefect, who left to join the S.A.T.C. [Tote Walker later returned to join the faculty to teach mathematics and lead Kent crews to victory at Henley many times.] Upon the red border of the Service Flag there were five gold stars — representing the Alumni who had given their lives in the service of their country. [In the spring of 1918, Robert Brinton Hill '10 was the first Kent man to die in battle, followed by his brother, Maurice McKnight Hill '13, in November.] In airplanes, on the field of battle, in sickness they died with courage, humility, and devotion: Charles McCormick '18, Livingston Wadsworth '17, and Frederick van Deusen '19. Later in the year

*Above: The Reverend Frederick
Herbert Sill, c. 1918.*

a sixth star appeared for Samuel H. Compton '13, who died of pneumonia after the Armistice." On November 22, 1918, Kent School joined the Town of Kent in a parade to celebrate peace. The "War to end all Wars" was over.

By the end of 1919, the school had grown to 154 boys in the second through sixth forms and 10 resident masters. The new study hall and the new library had been completed. The self-help system that began on that first night in 1906 had become a model for such systems in other schools. Kent graduates were already making a name for themselves and their beloved school, among them Roger Sessions '11 and Robert Hillyer '13, who were on their way to prominence in careers that would earn them Pulitzer Prizes in their fields, music and poetry.

And so those first challenging, exciting, and sometimes sorrowful years in the life of Kent ended. Miss Lizzy Fuller had been wrong; Kent School had survived and grown. The young Father Sill's dream had become reality.

Right: The main quad in 1913.

THE MOST UNFORGETTABLE CHARACTER I'VE MET

By Anson Gardner

LIKE THE OTHER 17 BOYS WHO STOOD NERVOUSLY BESIDE me that September afternoon in 1906 at Kent, Conn., I stared in openmouthed disbelief at the old farmhouse. It was the entire equipment of the new boarding school where we were to be the first class. One of the three teachers at hand haltingly announced that there were no books, that the furniture had not yet arrived and that the rent was paid only through the month. Just then the rickety old front door opened and out came the young monk who was to be our headmaster: the Rev. Frederick Herbert Sill, O.H.C. (the Episcopal Order of the Holy Cross). Sill was just 32, short and slight, with a frank, boyish face and stringy, straw-colored hair plastered so flat against his forehead that it looked almost painted on. His monastic habit resembled a billowing white nightgown, topped with a broad shoulder cowl that flapped like a hen's wings when he flailed his arms to emphasize a point.

"Welcome to Kent School," he said heartily. "There are no beds yet, but there are some mattresses on the floor." He spoke without the slightest concern over the physical limitations. Later that day when the cook was taken ill and could not prepare supper, Father Sill simply pointed a strong, stubby finger at several of us and assigned us the job of handling dishes. Then he swept into the kitchen, white wings flapping, and somehow concocted a creditable meal. Thus was inaugurated the Kent "Self-Help System"—and the boys have been waiting on table and performing all other housekeeping tasks except cooking and laundry ever since.

So contagious was the radiant enthusiasm of this odd white apparition, often referred to later as "The Great White Tent," that we assembled that night in our pajamas and gave him the first of untold thousands of Kent cheers that were to ring up and down the lovely Housatonic River Valley. Then we trooped confidently off to the hard mattresses on the creaking floors. The Kent way of life had begun.

Barely four months before that unique "Opening Day," Father Sill had received permission from his order to found a school. He had written a prospectus stating his aim: "to provide at minimum cost, for boys of exceptional ability and character, a combined academic

Reprinted from the *Reader's Digest*, January, 1961

and commercial course. *Simplicity of life, self-reliance and directness of purpose* are to be especially encouraged."

With characteristic candor, he had mailed this prospectus to 1500 well-to-do men, requesting a total of $250,000. He received exactly six answers and $300. When his father superior stopped by to commiserate on the failure of the enterprise, he was astounded to see that the young priest had no intention of quitting. Instead, Father Sill said cheerfully, "Well, if the Lord wants me to make a school with $300, I will do it."

My family had known this man long before I was shipped off to Kent, and I had heard many stories about him. He had been brought up on the lower West Side of Manhattan, where his father was vicar of St. Chrysostom's Chapel, originally founded over a saloon. Rubbing elbows with the poor, he learned early to respect pennies but never to worship dollars. His decision to enter the ministry did not come until after graduation from Columbia College, where he had been coxswain of the crew and editor of the magazine. He was hiking in Europe when a friend, Harrington Littell, later Bishop of Honolulu, asked him why he did not go into the ministry.

"I think I will," replied young Sill. It was as simple as that.

Once "Pater" (as we later came to call him) committed himself to a job, he hung on like a bulldog. How he hated an alibi of any sort! One bitterly cold night that first year at Kent, the main pipe froze and there was no water. "Good!" we boys thought. We would be able to sneak a few more minutes in our beds (finally arrived), since it was obvious that we could not brush our teeth or wash.

Not a bit of it! At the usual time next morning that thunderous voice was heard echoing through the ancient hallways. "Everybody *out*! Everybody *out!*" We were to form a bucket brigade to the nearby well. If the water would not come to us, then we would go to the water.

That winter, crisis followed crisis—like the time Pater bounced into the dining room, holding up a note. "Well, fellows," he said, "no more coal on credit." By this time, financial dilemmas were as familiar to us as algebra, and we eagerly awaited the solution. Pater

simply asked for volunteers, and soon he had us out in the woods cutting firewood until the budget was balanced. He even made a profit——by selling surplus logs for use as railroad ties.

We had no business manager in those days. Later, as the school expanded to more than 100 boys and this office became necessary, Pater could never refrain from passing along graphic little tips on frugality. One day a teacher discovered the first dignified holder of that job sitting at his desk piling wooden matches in little pyramids. "What kind of game is that?" the teacher asked.

"It's no game," came the disgruntled reply. "I'm counting the fool things. Sill says we can save money by figuring which brand gives us the most matches per box. And, by golly, he's right!"

To a man who practiced such frugality no expenditure seemed too great, however, where a boy's well-being was involved. "Telephone me, *collect*" he told graduating boys who, he felt, might hit snags at college, "at any hour of the day or night when you're in trouble." Over the years, the cost of these "trouble calls" ran to thousands of dollars.

Pater was acutely sensitive to the unique needs of boys with special talents, as poet Robert Hillyer noted when he wrote me recently: "He had the insight and wisdom to let an imaginative boy like me follow his own devices apart from organized athletics and groups—a dispensation for which I express gratitude to this day."

Pater's abiding love for his boys sometimes led him to superb acts of self-sacrifice. On Thanksgiving Day, 1938, he led the school in joyous celebration of a holiday that has always been most meaningful at Kent. He mingled throughout the morning with all the boys—especially with those who were unused to holidays away from home. Then he quietly left for his family's home, without revealing what he had known since early dawn: that his mother had died suddenly during the night.

Nothing ever abashed this man. Before a football game, astonished visitors frequently saw his familiar white form, robe hitched up under a waist cord, crouching on the side lines opposite some hulking lineman. There, with black cross dangling at his neck, thin bare legs sticking up out of oversized, scuffed black shoes, he would shout so loudly you could hear him the length of the stands: "Block *hard'*. Like this." Then he would lunge furiously, graphically getting his point across. A few hours later this same white figure would be seen kneeling in chapel, in deep meditation.

Pater was always being pestered by parents who thought his ideas of exercise far too rigorous. (He insisted on outdoor activity every day, whatever the weather.) "I fixed one griping parent," he told me gleefully once. "I didn't say a word. I just handed the man a copy of the school's annual medical report. For the entire preceding school year our medical expenses had come to an average of $2.50 per boy!"

During the first 15 years of Kent, Pater himself coached the hockey squad—although he could not even stand up on skates. The teams were highly successful. Tackling assignments like this was just one of the many ways in which Pater taught his personal belief that almost anything can be accomplished through vitality, enterprise and determination. And this spirit pervaded the classroom as well as the playing field. In study hall, for example, he permitted no teachers to squander their talents as watchdogs. "Why use *Ovid* to prop a window that stays open by itself?" he would say.

"Besides, Anson," he once informed me, "this method saves the school at least two teachers a year, in terms of time."

Self-reliance was not, of course, always easy to instill. One fall day he came upon a new boy sobbing in a hallway, a case of acute homesickness. He wrapped a white-mantled arm around the boy's shoulder and walked him gently up to the musty, slope-walled, picture-lined attic he called his study. "Do you want to go home?" he asked.

"I guess so," the boy replied tearfully.

Pater reached into the depths of his robe, among the old pipe, small Bible and alumni directory he habitually carried, and pulled out ten dollars. "Here. The train for New York comes through tomorrow at nine. You can take it, if you like."

All at once the boy found himself placed, in a not unkindly way, on his own, free to make a decision. Mysteriously (to the boy, but not to Pater), the homesickness vanished. That was 35 years ago. The "boy"

is still at Kent—a respected member of the faculty.

A Columbia classmate of Pater's once said to him, "Fred, how did you ever get *sidetracked* into teaching?"

"If you only knew," Pater said, "the daily joy of my life, and the added joy of knowing men who look upon Kent as a part of home, you would consider *yourself* on a siding, while I whirl through on a fast express."

It was a "fast express," all right. Day after day the light flicked on in Pater's austere little room at 5:30 a.m., the hour he arose for meditation. He would then plunge into activities that rarely let up before midnight. One consequence was that by the 1930s the school had grown from the original old farmhouse into a lovely cluster of Georgian buildings grouped around a handsome Norman chapel. And boys were coming from all over the United States to share the Kent way of life.

Meanwhile, beyond the confines of his own campus, Pater was making significant contributions to all independent secondary-school education by organizing open-forum discussions on teaching and discipline. He was instrumental, too, in founding the International Schoolboy Fellowship in 1928, and thereafter was active in bringing English, German and other foreign students to the United States on an exchange basis.

Also, Pater accomplished more than any other man in the country for schoolboy rowing. He introduced crew as a sport at Kent shortly after World War I, using a revamped chicken coop as a boathouse. Only five years later the Kent varsity crew competed at the famed Henley Regatta in England. In 1933 came the proud moment when a Sill-coached crew won the Thames Challenge Cup, an achievement repeated by Kent crews three times since.

In 1940, at the age of 66, Pater suffered the first of a series of paralyzing strokes that forced him to retire from the headmaster's chair to a wheel chair. All of us who knew him wondered then whether his faith might be dimmed, his spirit shaken. Our fears vanished the first day he was wheeled into the chapel to take his place with the boys after a long absence. His face was radiant with utter faith.

During the 12 years between the first stroke and his death, Pater uttered never a word of complaint. In the late afternoons, one of his special joys was to listen to another unique and significant innovation of his: the tower bells. When the peal had been offered to him as a gift for the new chapel, Pater had been advised that no young boys could ever swing the heavy bells (one of them weighed 1500 pounds), even under the tutelage of a professional bell-ringer. Pater proved the advisers wrong: when the bell-ringer finally retired, Kent boys were able to hand down the training and tradition from class to class, and last Easter six Kent students performed the rare demonstration of completing the first ringing of a quarter peal in the United States in 25 years. On my last visit before his death in 1952, Pater seemed to know that the end was near. With half-paralyzed lips trying to communicate what was behind the still vibrant sparkle in his eyes, he brought back to mind a vivid picture of that first preposterous day at Kent in 1906. By all the laws of logic and economics, that school should not have survived. Yet here we were, surrounded by his magnificent accomplishment. No one had reckoned with his utter faith in God and the strength of his three inspired precepts: *simplicity of life, self-reliance and directness of purpose.*

After a successful business career in charge of the foreign operations of the American Machine and Foundry Co., Anson Gardner returned to Kent School to serve for five years as director of admissions. He retired from this post in 1959.

II
REWARDS OF FAITH

W ILLIAM WORTHINGTON '24, WHO BECAME A HISTORY MASTER AT Kent, described the School as it was in the early '20s probably providing a fairly accurate picture of the School as it was in its first three decades once it had settled into the pattern established by Father Sill. Students arrived by train for the most part, some coming up from New York City, some down from Pittsfield. The first chapel of the year was held on the day they arrived, and the Kent hymn "Oh Savior, Precious Savior" was sung and the School scripture, Philippians II: 5-10, was read. Chapel was followed by dinner and later bedtime. Worthington wrote:

"I suppose everyone who has graduated from Kent feels that the school has changed drastically since he first went there, and I will try to give a picture of the Kent that I was introduced to in 1920. Physically it was a collection of wooden buildings. The windows had small panes, and there were green shutters on them all. As you crossed the bridge from town—a wrought iron structure with two trusses supported by a stone pier in the middle—you came to a road which ran across the bridge road, and ahead was a field. To the right the dirt road led to the football field and the Field House. To the left the road led to the school buildings. This was the main road to Macedonia and to New York State. As you walked up it, you passed a half dozen tennis courts on the right, and on the left a garden with cabbages, Brussels sprouts, melons, and corn, and beyond it you came to the Alumni House, the Study Hall, the North Building, and the Main Building. If you passed to the left, behind this you came to the chapel and beyond it to the barn. The Infirmary was directly behind the Main Building. Aside from a few masters' cottages and the farmer's cottage down the river, that was the school."

He described the daily schedule in the fall and winter – and presumably the spring.

6:00 AM	Voluntary Chapel
6:15	Rising Bell
6:45	Breakfast (Between end of breakfast and 7:45 everyone made his bed, cleaned his room, and did his "job" of housekeeping.)

Above left: Father Sill, 1920. Above right: The football field and Field House.

7:45	Job Assembly
8:15–10:30	First three periods for classes
10:30	Recess
10:45–12:15	Two more class periods
12:20	Lunch
1:15–3:15	Sports, etc.
3:45–6:15	Job Assembly, followed by final three class periods
6:20	Chapel, followed immediately by supper
7:30–8:30	Night Study
9:00	Lights for everyone but sixth formers.

Everyone was expected to be bathed and dressed for chapel and dinner, including wearing a stiff collar and a suit by the afternoon job assembly.

Night study was attended by everyone but the sixth form and those excused because of good academic standing. Marks were posted on Friday so that the boys could report them to their parents in their weekly letter, written on Sundays. *The Kent News* regularly reported the marks of those whose grades were 80% or more. On Saturday night the marks were read out in assembly, the honor roll for the week was read, and the out-of-study list announced. Following this came the speechmaking. All third, fourth, and fifth formers took turns delivering a speech to the school, and Fr. Sill would announce the speakers for the next week at the end of the Saturday meeting. The sixth formers took notes, and one of them would be asked to review, comment on, and criticize the speeches, assuring their attention.

Obviously, in the late '20s and early '30s some of this changed. Worthington wrote that the importance of the speeches declined over the years, and he mentions that marks were given out during his first two years (1920-

Left: North building and study hall in 1920.

1922) at Kent. The best part of that, it would seem, was that every Monday night there was an "Over-Eighty Feed." "All the boys on the honor roll were invited to the [Headmaster's] study at 8:30 to partake of soda crackers and whatever could be concocted to drink out of hot water, loose tea, milk, and ordinary cocoa. It was not very filling, but fun, because Pater was always there to joke and talk, and we were allowed to stay up until 10 o'clock."

Afternoon sports in the fall were football primarily. It was organized into a First and Second team, both of which played other schools. The boys

Left: The Kent School faculty, 1921.
First row: Harrington, Schiedt, Fr. Sill,
Cuthbertson, Voorhees. Second row: Nadal,
Blackman, Humphreys, Johnson, Evans,
Anders, Hilliard, Charlier, Walker.

Above left: Father Sill, 1921
Above right: Pater in his study.

below the second team level were divided into two leagues, a junior league of those over 120 lbs., and a midget league of those under 120 lbs. Finally, "the spring of 1922 marked a great watershed in Kent's history. Fr. Sill's dream of having an eight-oared crew came to fruition." And while this story deserves a place of its own in any history of Kent, some of the circumstances surrounding its advent, as reported by Bill Worthington, should probably be mentioned here.

> To me, unknowing, the beginning of this change came one day when, as an honor-roll scholar, I was given a work-holiday and told to report to Archie Wing the farmer at the hen house. Here we caught and beheaded all the remaining hens, carried their corpses to the old pig pen next door, where we dunked them in a boiling caldron and plucked them. The school had chicken fricassee the next Saturday for the fourth week in a row. I have never been sure whether the decision to switch the henhouse into a boat house began with a realization that the hen business was not profitable, or because Pater suddenly realized that if we ate the hens all up there would be a place to store a couple of shells. At any rate the house was moved closer to the river, and extended somewhat in length; two old shells, gifts from the New York Boat Club, arrived in a day coach which the local freight switched off onto what was called Nolan's Siding in Kent, and groups of boys took turns carrying them out.

     Maitland Edey '28, in an article written for the Winter 1983 *Quarterly*, began his "recollections," saying "We were not an outstanding class. The one

ahead of us was larger, so was the one after us. Both produced better records in the sports that counted: football, hockey, and crew. Both went to Henley, we did not. Both were more highly regarded by Father Sill. . . ."

With almost nothing to read but school books, and little else in the way of extra-curricular activities provided, we manufactured our own amusements. Fads would sweep through the school from time to time. When I was a third former several of us made cardboard roulette wheels and began gambling, using thumb tacks as currency. In no time the stationery store was sold out of thumb tacks, and a bright second former named Bridgman had ten or twenty thousand of them. We also climbed and explored a lot, walked up Mt. Algo and Numeral Mountain. There were caves in the rocks up there, which we made into dens. But, for most of us, most of our time was spent at sports: the form teams, the leagues, and the school teams. There were always touch football games being played, using swollen old footballs from a supply kept in the field house. When the football season ended, members of the varsity would join those pickup games, and their level of proficiency would escalate dramatically. Masters and coaches would also play: Bill Nadal, Ted Evans, Toto Walker. One year the fad was cross-country touch football. One goal was the entrance to the bridge over the Housatonic. The other was the entrance to the school farm, half a mile away. There were no sidelines, and most of

those games were waged on the slopes of the mountains, with a crowd of players maneuvering below while the man with the ball scrambled higher and higher to outflank the opposition and come sliding down nearer the goal.

Edey also provides a first-hand account of the epidemic that struck the school in the winter of '27-'28. "My last winter at Kent was one that tried the school to its very soul. A virulent infection struck it, hospitalizing boys almost faster than room could be made for them. I was hit in due course. Feeling very sick one morning, I went to the infirmary, but because of the crisis condition there I was told to go back to my room and spend the day in bed. I did, but by evening I scarcely knew where I was, and remember only being carried down the study hall stairs on a stretcher as the rest of the school was pouring in for evening assembly. The next days were a blur. I was in a private room somewhere in the infirmary, confused that the chapel bell was ringing at odd times of the day. Father Sill would come in and pray at the end of my bed. I asked him about the bells, and he could only shake his head, the tears running down his face, unwilling to explain that they were funeral services for dead boys.

"That was an agonizing time for the Old Man, and must have tested his faith to its very core. Five boys died that winter, one of them our classmate Charlie Gunn, but a number of others, though desperately ill, survived. That must have been a great restorative to him. . . ."

The winter was over, and spring again came to the valley, bringing with it Prize Day.

"We clustered in front of the chapel steps to compare diplomas – in gray wrappers with blue and gray silk ribbons, each written out in his own hand by the Old Man, each different, each a personal communication to the recipient, a last idiosyncratic message to every boy from the man who had so

THE ORIGINAL COAT OF ARMS

In 1927 Father Sill asked Robert Symonds, a close friend of the school, to create a coat of arms for Kent School. The job required a great deal of research in order to get the Sill Coat of Arms from England and to create a pattern suitable for narrating the history of Kent School. After long hours of work, Mr. Symonds created the Coat of Arms, which now hangs over the fireplace in the Headmaster's Study. The description which follows appeared in the *Kent News* in April 1929.

On the base of the Sill arms was added CHI RHO which symbolized the part which the Order of the Holy Cross had in the founding of Kent. Under CHI RHO, the School motto of Simplicity of Life, Self-reliance, Directness of Purpose is carved in the Latin terms Temperantia, Fiducia, and Constantia. There is on the top of the shield, which is in the middle of the Coat of Arms, a lion signifying war-like courage . . . [but also] a willingness to die for what is right. The helmet engraved over the shield was a real part of the Sill Coat of Arms and over that there is carved a golden dragon with wings. On close observation a Kent pennant can be seen flying over the head of the dragon. All this artistically designed figure is laid on a background of blue. It links together the Sill family, the Order of the Holy Cross and courage, all elements in the founding of Kent.

One amendment might be made to this description, as the creature described above as a dragon is really a griffin, a mythological beast with the head and wings of an eagle and the body of a lion.

The Latin motto is translated as Simplicity of Life, Self-Reliance, and Directness of Purpose. In an article written in February 1977, Gray Maxwell pointed out that "these words are the lay corollaries of the monastic vows of Poverty, Obedience, and Chastity, but this appears to be coincidental. Father Sill was responsible for the English equivalent of the motto which curiously preceded the Latin." Evidently it was Robert Symonds who transcribed the English words into the Latin.

In recent years, the Coat of Arms has been modernized, modified, and simplified, but the basic elements are still there, the lion for courage and a willingness to die for what is right and the *Chi Rho*, symbolic of the connection with the Order of the Holy Cross at the School's founding and of the Latin words *Christus Rex*, Christ the King. The seal has three main parts: the lion in *gules* (red), the "fess fretty," the belt that divides the seal in two, in *sable* and *or* (black and gold), and the *Chi Rho*, also in *gules*. These are on a background of *argent* (silver). At the bottom is the School's motto in Latin.

Above left: The infirmary and the RAD House.
The infirmary was the first brick building of
Fr. Sill's "permanent Kent."
Above right: Study hall under St. Joseph's Chapel.

powerfully affected his life for three, four, or five years. That diploma, it seems to me, encapsulates everything that was best and worst about Kent. It was a one-man school from start to finish, run by a peculiar but inspired man, one in which every boy had a personal relationship with that man. The relationship may not have been a good one. It may have been based on fear and avoidance— as mine was—but there was nothing phony or institutionalized or plastic about it. It was real. No boy in the 1920s succeeded in getting through Kent without being affected strongly by it. I am not sure other schools of the time could claim that. Their diplomas were factory-made, identical except for the recipient's hand-lettered name. They lacked that last capricious touch, the Old Man's own assessment of what he thought of you as a boy. Reading mine, I discovered with great surprise that he had apparently kept a closer eye on me than I had ever imagined. My thought had been that I had slid unnoticed through the school. Not so. He *knew* me. When that day ended I felt a little bigger than I had when it started."

There was no doubt. Kent and Father Sill were one.

Unlike many schools, Kent does not have a building named for its founder, no Sill Hall, not even a Founder's Hall. (The Boathouse, while dedicated to Father Sill, is never called the Sill Boathouse. The only direct reference to the founder there is the Sill Oar, which stands in front of the building.) There is no statue of Father Sill to greet visitors to the campus. His grave in the Chapel garden is marked by a simple wooden cross, and there are no formal pilgrimages to it, not even on the Feast of St. Michael and All Angels. His portrait hangs over the fireplace in the Dining Hall, and no doubt passersby take note of it and of the portraits of three other headmasters that hang on the north wall. But if we seek a monument, Father Sill's sons and daughters like the son of Christopher Wren, the great architect of St. Paul's Cathedral in London, might well say *Si monumentum requires circumspice,* if you would see the man's monument, look around.

From the beginning, Father Sill envisioned "the permanent Kent," a school of fireproof buildings that would serve its students well. In 1923, that dream began to come to fruition with the completion of the Infirmary on the present site of Case Dormitory. It was the first brick building on the campus, and the first fireproof one. It was followed the next year by the Dining Hall, the old section, wood paneled, tall glass windows looking out at Old Main, which stood across from where the Administration Building stands today. The wooden St. Joseph's stood to its right, where Schoolhouse is now located. It is easy to see exactly where it was because there was, and is, a birch tree with a rather idiosyncratic branch reaching out toward the river, the tree under which students like to sit to visit with each other today. The state road, paved by 1925, still cut through the campus. The next year the new administration building was completed and dedicated. The building included a new Headmaster's Study, dedicated in memory of Adrian Van Tapscott '41, and Alumni rooms, dedicated in memory of John Dryden. In its article about the dedication, the *Kent News* commented that "the completion and dedication of the New Administration Building which will be known as the New Main Building marks the final step in the completion of the Permanent Kent which Pater began in 1906." Little did they know!

In 1928, a medical clinic containing an apartment for the school doctor opened following the epidemic of 1927-28, which caused the deaths of five Kent boys. That building, called the RAD House in honor of Robert Alfred Davison, houses the deans' offices today. Davison, Father Sill's cousin, died in the summer of 1911 before he could fulfill his dream of coming to Kent. When the building was opened, the clinic itself was named for Robert N. Ogden (formerly '29) who had died in the streptococcus epidemic the previous year. Originally the building stood next to the Infirmary, but when the boys and girls campuses were consolidated, it was moved, slowly, past Schoolhouse, inches separating it from that building and the stone retaining wall

Below left: The RAD House, given by his parents in memory of Robert Alfred Davison, an enrolled member of the class of 1916, who died in August 1911 after having been accepted for admission to Kent the following fall. Dedicated in 1928.

Below right: A portrait of Father Sill in 1930.

Above: North Dormitory in 1930.

along the river road, to its present location, forming a quadrangle with Schoolhouse, the Administration Building, and Middle Dorm South.

The next decade of Kent's life saw enormous changes. On the afternoon of May 14, 1930, Father Sill turned the first spadeful of earth to break ground for the new St. Joseph's Chapel and North Dormitory. *The Kent News* reported the occasion.

"The first part of the ceremony took place in the Chapel, where Father Sill, accompanied by his servers, who were the prefects for 1930 and 1931, read that portion of the Bible which tells of Solomon's first steps in undertaking to build the temple. After several prayers had been said, the congregation filed out and proceeded to the site of the new dormitory, just below where Mr. Nadal's cottage formerly stood. Father Sill and the servers led the procession, with the guests and Faculty following. After them came the boys of the school by their forms, the Sixth Form leading.

"When all had assembled around the chosen spot, Fr. Sill repeated several prayers and then made a short address. . . . He said that as this new building was for the use of the youngest boys of the School, and that these had been housed since the start in what is familiarly known as the North Dorm, that it had been decided to call this new building the North Dormitory. He expressed the hope that the men engaged in labor on this building—the bricklayers, the masons, and the carpenters—would be protected by God from any harm which might befall them while erecting the building.

"When he had finished his address, Fr. Sill took up the spade and turned over the first spade full. . . .

"Fr. Sill and the servers, followed by the spectators, then went over to the Form House Hill, where the new Chapel is to be built. When all had gathered around the site, the Headmaster said several prayers, asking for the Lord's guidance in the undertaking and His protection for all those engaged in work upon it. . . .

"The last part of the ceremony was then carried out, when Fr. Sill, followed by the servers, walked around the site, blessing the ground."

Father Sill called on Mr. Harmon, who drew up the plans for North Dormitory; his son; Mr. Evans, who had been master of the old North dormitory; and the 1931 Senior Prefect, Charles Colmore, to assist in breaking ground for North. The architect of the chapel, Mr. Roger Bullard; his sons, Henry and Roger; Randolph Titus '09, Business Manager of the School and representative of the Alumni; and Garret Goodbody, the retiring Senior Prefect, who represented the boys, assisted in breaking ground for the chapel. Arvid E.

Taube, Chairman of the Alumni Chapel Fund was unable to be present but sent a congratulatory telegram.

Later that year, the cornerstone of the new chapel was laid in a ceremony attended by over five hundred people, including the Rt. Reverend Chauncey Brewster, Bishop of Connecticut, and Fr. Hughson, Superior of the Order of the Holy Cross. Both North Dorm and St. Joseph's Chapel were completed in 1931.

The story of the beautiful St. Joseph's Chapel that we know today, though, really begins in 1927, in a rather surprising way. Thumbing through the Kent News *issue dated 9 November of that year, one learns that Father Sill had just received plans and elevations for a proposed new chapel at Kent School. They came from his young friend Dillingham Palmer, of the class of 1920, who had gone on to Yale and just recently finished a three-year stint as a graduate student there with an M.F.A. in architecture. Presumably the plans and drawings were his thesis project.*

It was characteristic of Father Sill to keep in touch with his recent alumni, and we know that on at least one occasion, in the fall of 1925, he had driven to New Haven with "Ding" Palmer. One wonders whether they discussed the architectural needs of the School on that trip, and what a new Kent School Chapel might look like, but posterity will never know. One gets the impression from his reaction to Palmer's proposal that in 1927 Father Sill hadn't thought much about a new chapel, but he certainly was very happy to now, and in his enthusiasm he called a special evening meeting at the School to show the plans to anyone who might wish to see them.

It is a great shame that these plans, as far as we know, have not survived. From the News *article we learn only that the "proposed chapel" was "to stand upon the Form House Hill, and to dominate the entire Kent Valley . . . [it would] face the river, overlooking the original buildings, and [it would] be very much larger than the simple but beautiful chapel in use at the present." In the rear would be a cloister leading to a tall tower, and the complex would be clad with heavy stone, presumably local field stone. The windows would be of colored glass, with special focus*

Above: Construction of the chapel roof.

on a *set of three windows above the altar at the east end. In other words, Dillingham Palmer basically chose the site, the orientation, and the architectural concept for the building that eventually got built, and he got to do this before he even finished graduate school! In view of his distinguished later career as an architect and a water colorist, though, it may be that young Palmer actually deserved this privilege.*

The institutional wheels didn't really start turning, however, until the fall of 1928, when Father Sill called a meeting of the five fathers of Kent boys who were architects, along with Frank Humphrey, the head of the Fathers' [i.e. Parents'] Association, to be held on Thanksgiving Day. To us this may seem like a strange time for a meeting, but we must realize there was no Thanksgiving vacation at Kent School in those days; the boys were not allowed to go home. Instead, it was a good time for parents to come and visit their sons, and apparently many of them did. The purpose of this meeting was to form a committee to consider what the physical needs of the School would be over the next several years, and who might be willing and able to contribute to meeting those needs professionally. The assembled group apparently agreed to make Arthur Loomis Harmon head of the committee, as he was a partner in the firm that was working on the Empire State Building at the time, and was obviously a distinguished professional architect. Roger Harrington

Right: North Dormitory in 1932.

Above: St. Joseph's Chapel from Schaghticoke in the 1930s.

Bullard, while being unassuming in manner, was also well liked and respected, and they agreed that he would be the committee secretary. It quickly became apparent that what the School needed first for the 25th anniversary in 1931 was a major new dormitory, to replace the existing wooden North Dormitory, and a really substantial chapel: Harmon was willing to take on the dormitory project, and Bullard, though he had never designed a church or chapel before, accepted the responsibility of planning and overseeing the construction of the new St. Joseph's.

They apparently discussed at some length what the general character of the chapel might be—for this they presumably started with Father Sill's stipulations and Dillingham Palmer's plans. Its architectural style would be Norman, reflecting the heritage of ecclesiastical architecture in England and France during the 11th and 12th centuries, the period when the great monastic movement of St. Bernard and so many others was in its heyday. Simplicity, strength, and austerity—as a monk Father Sill by temperament preferred those qualities, but he also believed they would set a good example for his boys.

The new chapel had to be able to seat three hundred, of whom seventy would be seniors in raised stalls down the sides and in the back: the seniors would be responsible for supervising the discipline of the younger boys assigned to seats in the regular rows. The north side would have an aisle which needed to be kept clear for liturgical processions, and also accommodate temporary seating for visitors. In the chancel would be facing stalls for the choir, with the organ console behind

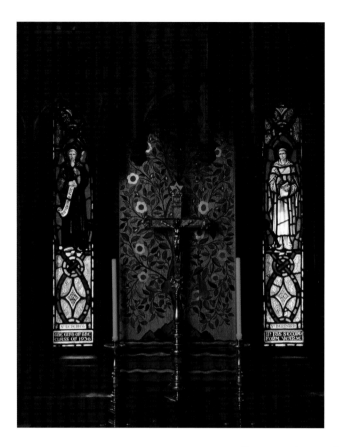

Above: Holy Cross Altar.

the stalls on the left (north) side. In the short south transept there would be an enclosed entrance and a small antechapel where monks from the Order of the Holy Cross who were currently teaching at the School could say their daily offices, according to the rule of discipline observed by the O.H.C. In the larger north transept there would be a small sacristy and a somewhat larger choir room downstairs, and a stairway leading up to an "upper room" for meetings and interviews, plus the door opening into the cloisters leading up to the bell-tower out back. From the beginning the bell-tower was intended to be much taller than the chapel roof, so it would have a commanding presence and be easily visible for some distance up and down the valley.

The whole complex would indeed be faced with local field-stone, for a couple of reasons: first of all, this stone would have an attractive warmth of color and grittiness of texture, exemplifying by its rugged simplicity the very virtue Father Sill wished to instill in his foster-children, the boys of the School. Furthermore, there was a large quantity of this stone piled up in stone walls all around the School, and elsewhere in the town of Kent, which could easily be collected, at minimal cost. All the contractors would have to do to get it would be to send a team of men around with a flat-bed truck, who would dismantle the stone walls scattered around the School and throw the stones up onto the truck. For architectural stone trim, however, they would use a different stone, which masons could carve more easily: Indiana limestone. This seemed to be the obvious choice, since it was being used so much those days for building large churches, such as the National Cathedral in Washington, D.C., St. Thomas Church in New York City, Princeton University Chapel, Cadet Chapel at West Point, Trinity College Chapel, and many others.

Architect Roger Bullard and his team worked on the plans through the winter of 1929, getting their staff artist, Schell Lewis, to paint a view from the southeast of the completed building as it was then projected, copies of which survive to this day. To a hasty glance, the Chapel as rendered looks pretty much the way it does today, but there are some small differences which are important.

Perhaps the most important of these design changes, subtle though they were, had to do with proportions, and they resulted from the good advice of another prominent architect, Philip Hubert Frohman. Frohman was a well-known specialist in medieval architecture, based in Washington, D.C., where he was overseeing the continuing work on the National Cathedral; he took issue with the overall squatness of the interior as planned, and got Bullard to make several important changes which would give the interior a greater sense of loftiness and space more authentically in keeping with the building's Norman antecedents. First, he got Bullard to increase the thickness of the massive piers down the sides of the nave to a full three feet, and the arcade springing from them to 3 ½ feet, for a greater sense of solidity in accordance with the Norman style. Second, Frohman got Bullard to raise the height of the piers some 3 ½ feet, to improve the proportions and give the interior enough spaciousness overhead to convey a sense of holy awe to those seated below. This would make the side walls higher, too, and provide enough height for stained-glass windows to have the most satisfying proportions. Also, the windows themselves should not be coupled, as in the original proposal, because that would be historically anachronistic, but they should be single, and in a Norman structure of this size they should only be about 18 inches wide. Too much light would spoil the dimness and vitiate the sense of mystery which such a building should convey. A further advantage to higher walls inside would be higher eaves outside, which would help prevent the roof from seeming to come down almost to the ground.

Third, citing the relatively narrow proportions of medieval cathedrals in England, Frohman got Bullard to narrow the span of the interior from 38' to 32': the result of this would not only be more satisfying proportions inside, but also, from the outside, a roof significantly less prominent and dominating.

Being a specialist in authentic medieval stone detailing, Frohman was able to help Bullard with the proper design of carved limestone capitals in the nave and cloisters, and other details elsewhere in the building as well. He could also discuss the iconography of the stained-glass windows with Father Sill, who already had a lot of ideas on the subject, and from his experience at the Cathedral in Washington recommend craftsmen who would be capable of producing stained-glass windows of the highest quality, in a historically authentic style.

Other changes to the 1929 design of the chapel that came out of discussions between these individuals were as follows: the double bell-cote at the peak of the roof at the east end was made single because there would be only one Sanctus bell, and it was moved to its present position over the chancel arch: here the bell-rope could be led down inside to a spot where a person could be handy to ring the bell at the prescribed time, at the moment of the consecration of the host during the mass. The service bell from the old chapel was too large to mount in a peak-of-the-roof bell-cote and be out of the weather, so a special dormer for it was planned inside the eastern slope of the north transept roof, with its rope accessible to student ringers near the foot of the main stairs. Another significant change was the addition of a stubby high south transept, to balance the north transept needed to provide space for an organ loft upstairs.

There were important changes in the fenestration: first of all, they decided to have only single 18-inch windows on the south side of the nave, because with the prevailing sun beaming in on that side, single windows there would provide about the same level of illumination that pairs of windows would provide in the north aisle. Second, in the east end, above the altar, they would not have a rose window, but rather a triple lancet window, as we see today. Third, the pairs of little windows in the sides of the chancel and in the so-called "antechapel" were separated, and additional plain windows were planned for upstairs in various places in both transepts. The empty room above the southeast entrance and antechapel was given two little windows in the pre-Norman Anglo-Saxon style, with their pointed tops formed by sloping stone slabs. Father Sill and his architect did this to suggest something of the stylistic complexity of many early medieval churches, which tended to get added-to over several centuries in whatever style was current at the particular moment. It could be argued that this was perhaps misconceived because historically the Anglo-Saxon style came first and would continue to show only in the lowest portions of the masonry, with later additions above done first in the Norman or Romanesque style and still later in Gothic—but no matter.

One notices, too, in Schell Lewis's rendition that there is an east-facing porch off the north transept which was never built, and also, the cloisters are different: the roof as built has a *pitch to it, and the buttresses have stone pinnacles which definitely add to the design. There are some minor differences in the bell-tower, too. Philip Frohman apparently preferred an English-Norman style for the tower rather than the French, with its pointed crest, but on that matter Mr. Bullard held firm. Needless to say, he had to re-do his plans rather extensively, and he was given until 15 January 1930 to accomplish this: the feeling was that on that schedule there would be plenty of time to put the plans out for competitive bids and engage the winning contractor before starting construction, which they would need to do no later than the following June.*

During the following months Father Sill conferred extensively with all the important individuals involved in this process—with not just the architects Bullard, Harmon and Frohman, but also his able business manager, "Bunny" Titus '09. He worked very closely with his Superior at West Park, Father Huntington, who was also chairman of the board for the School and a close friend; he also connected with Frank Humphrey, head of the Parents' Association, who was a successful international banker on Wall Street and who could provide both directly and indirectly a lot of help with the financing. Humphrey was a colleague and good friend of Lord Rothermere, of London, who incidentally had recently been enough of a friend of the School to donate new rowing shells to the Kent crews who went to race at Henley in 1927 and 1929. It was Humphrey, a frequent traveler to the U.K., who realized that the proposed bell-tower at Kent would accommodate a large English 'ring' of bells for change-ringing, and the foundry for producing it was right there in East London: Mears and Stainbank, now generally known as the Whitechapel Bell Foundry.

The final impetus for his making this happen came in the spring of 1929, after Mrs. Humphrey and their young son, Robert, boarded the liner Paris in New York to join him in London. They had no sooner started out when the boy developed a serious case of double mastoiditis, and apparently there was no doctor on the ship who was capable of dealing with it. Suddenly they were very concerned for young Robert's life: they needed to get him to a hospital ashore, and there was no way to do that. According to an article in the New York Times the next thing that happened was that the ship's pilot—who most certainly should have known better—managed to steer the large vessel into a mud-bank off the side of the channel, and there she stuck fast. While the shipping company scrambled first to get the ship off—without success—and then to off-load onto a lighter alongside enough hundreds of tons of coal to lighten the ship so she'd float off, they were able to get the sick boy and his mother onto a small boat and whisk him off to a hospital ashore—conceivably saving his life. When Humphrey got wind of this, it seemed nothing less than a miracle of divine intervention, and he resolved to give a set of ten large Whitechapel bells to the School as a thank-offering. There just remained the details of contracting with Mr. Hughes at the Foundry to do the work, to get to him the interior dimensions of the proposed tower, and to see that architect Bullard understood what structural details needed to be incorporated into the tower, in order to accommodate the physical arrangement of the heavy bells in their frame, their considerable weight, and the structural vibration induced by their swinging repeatedly around and back when in use.

At this time, in 1929, there was only one place in America where English change-ringing was being actively pursued, and that was high up in the west-end tower of the lovely Chapel at the Groton School: to this day the visitor to the ringing chamber there can see the plaques on the wall and realize that a unique and distinguished tradition of change-ringing started

there back in the 19ᵗʰ century, and in the 1920s was going strong. Groton has 10 lovely bells, just like Kent, but Kent's are heavier, and one can't help wondering if back in 1929 Humphrey knew all this and deliberately planned larger bells in order to do the long-established competitor school one better!

In any case, the Whitechapel people were surprised and delighted to get the business, and apparently to cast the Kent bells they used molds taken from the bells they had recently hung in the free-standing stone tower looking down the hill-side at the chancel of ancient St. David's Cathedral in Wales.

For the stained-glass windows consulting architect Frohman recommended two firms which had contributed authentically medieval-style windows to the National Cathedral: James Powell and Sons in London, and Clement Heaton on Long Island. After discussions Father Sill decided to get the Powell studio to do a set of four windows high up on the sides of the chancel, and Heaton to do most of the rest: the three lancets above the altar, and the twelve windows down the sides of the nave. All the windows in the chancel would use full color, and depict persons significant to the School: in the east wall above the altar, the central lancet would have the Virgin Mary offering the boy Jesus, the smaller lancet on the left would show St. Joseph, and the one on the right would show St. Louis. Father Sill considered these two to be the patron saints of the School: Joseph, the foster-father of Jesus, just as he himself would be foster-father to the boys entrusted to his care, and Louis, because it was while he had been conducting a mission for the O.H.C. in St. Louis that he received his call, and received permission from his Superior, to start up a boys school. These three windows above the altar would be in the style of the great 13ᵗʰ-century windows in Chartres Cathedral. The four side windows in the chancel, by the Powell studio, would depict four saints chosen to correspond with the four activities of boys at the School: St. Stephen with worship,

Left: Bell casting.

Above: The Triptych at the east end over the altar.

St. Andrew with the jobs program (he is depicted chopping wood), St. John with study, and St. Lawrence with sports—specifically crew, dear to Father Sill's heart.

In the nave, with the exception of the rose window, the windows would be much more muted in color, because Father Sill wanted the boys' focus to be up front in the chancel; he and Clement Heaton chose grisaille glass, which has an overall grayish effect due to the areas of dark grey-brown vitreous paint applied in cross-hatching, and fused into the glass by re-firing. There would be some beautifully colored geometric patterns, to be sure, but no subject matter; these windows, interestingly, have nothing specifically religious about them, only the Latin words of the Kent School motto: Temperantia, Constantia, and Fiducia—dubiously back-translated from the English "Simplicity of life, Self-reliance, and Directness of purpose." The only depictions in the grisaille windows would be the coats-of-arms of the honorees and/or donors, when appropriate. The exception to this iconography would be the two windows in the north aisle, above the side-altar in honor of Father Sill's late friend and brother in the monastery, Father Allen, who had recently died on a mission to Africa. These would have color, and depict Sts. Dominick and Augustine, patron saints of the O.H.C.

Father Sill gave a lot of thought to the windows of St. Joseph's, and when he received the "cartoons" or mock-up drawings for them, he checked them carefully. He took issue with the first versions of the saints' faces, considering them sickly and contemptible, and made their designers do them over, to make the saints manly enough for growing boys to look up to. The cult of athletic manhood was alive and well at Kent in those days!

There survives in the School archives to this day some of the official correspondence between the various individuals involved in the process of conceptualizing, designing, and eventually erecting this Chapel: Father Sill and "Bunny" Titus '09 (the School's able Business Manager during this period), the architects Bullard and Frohman, Frank Humphrey (head of the Parents' Association) and a number of others. (Chapel history by Thomas Holcombe)

In a speech given to the annual Alumni Reunion in 1965, Henry W. Bragdon '24, born in 1906 himself, spoke of Father Sill (*Kent News*, April 26, 1980).

My father believed in reincarnation, and he had a notion about Father Sill that perhaps justifies the belief. He thought that Pater was a reincarnated Norman Abbot, who in a previous life had built a great school and a great abbey, surrounding it with meadows and farmlands taken from his neighbors. A great churchman, yes, but also a builder, a businessman, and a soldier who fought with a mace instead of a sword because it was against the laws of the Church to shed blood. A sinner, yes, but one who somehow believed that the good Lord would look out for him who had built altars and chapels to the glory of God and of his saints who had trained a whole generation of priests. And to pursue this thought, it is interesting that when Pater finally got the funds, he built in the center of his school a simple chapel, uncompromisingly Norman, to express his uncomplicated, direct faith. St. Joseph's Chapel is a fitting symbol of a man who was, for all his faults, a great builder, a great teacher, and a great priest.

This was not the end of building in the '30s, however. The Auditorium, now Schoolhouse, was completed in 1937, and in 1939 the Library Building, now Middle Dorm, replaced the old North Building and the study hall. When one considers that the fund raising and construction of these buildings occurred during the Great Depression, it becomes even more amazing that so much was done, and it attests to Father Sill's ability to share his vision for the Permanent Kent with others.

In the 1920s and 1930s Kent was growing in other ways, too. Robert Frost paid a visit in May 1920; Otey Berkeley '12 became the first Kent alumnus to be ordained; and, perhaps less momentous at the time but foreshadowing the future, the first daughter (after 11 sons) was born to a Kent alumnus on May 17, 1920.

Kent had more offspring, these of an academic sort. On May 31, 1923, Samuel Slater Bartlett '18 and Richard Cuyler '18 announced that they were establishing another school along the same lines as Kent. The new school would be located in South Kent, and its first session would begin in September 1923. Actually, Father Sill had purchased the land and helped to raise funds for the

Above: The four windows on the north and south walls of the sanctuary depict the four major aspects of Kent life: academics, chapel, jobs and athletics. St. John (top) and St. Stephen (bottom). Left: Details from the four windows.

new school, and was instrumental in choosing Bartlett and Cuyler to serve as Headmaster and Assistant Headmaster. Both men had been prefects at Kent, and, as a *Kent News* editorial said, "There are none more capable of carrying on this work than the two who are to have charge of it, Samuel Bartlett and Richard Cuyler, prefects both, who love and understand the least detail." South Kent School did indeed open on September 26, 1923, with an enrollment of 30 boys. Nine years later, in 1932, Paul Squibb '14 founded the Midland School in California. Midland, too, was founded along the lines of Kent, with a jobs program, a sliding tuition scale, prefects, and a farm. If anything, Midland was even more Spartan than Kent, for there was no electricity, and when a building

Above: St. Andrew (top) and St. Lawrence (bottom).
Above right: The rose window, St. Michael.
Right: The Father Allen altar: Saints Dominic and Augustine windows.

was needed, the boys built it. And, in 1941, Walter W. Littell '28 founded St. Luke's School in Webberville Texas, eleven miles east of Austin. St. Luke's, like Kent, had a self-help program, and its intention of maintaining simplicity of life aided it in keeping the expense to parents low, with a sliding tuition scale. Father Sill served on the school's advisory board.

The first members of the Kent chapter of the Cum Laude Society were installed on June 4, 1930. The summer of 1933 saw Kent's undefeated crew win the Thames Challenge Cup at Henley, and in 1936 the British-American Exchange Program, which began in 1928 with Father Sill's idea of a scholarship scheme associated with the English-Speaking Union in London, became fully operational. Kent's story had crossed the Atlantic, and it was clear that the voice of the school on the banks of the Housatonic was being heard from land to land.

The end of the 1930s saw the end of the Great Depression but also the beginning of war in Europe with the invasion of Poland in 1939. Gradually, as Sir Edward Gray, the British Foreign Secretary in 1914, said in that dark year, "the lights were going out all over Europe," and it was only a matter of time until the United States would enter the war.

For Kent, too, change was coming. On Prize Day 1941, Father William S. Chalmers became Kent School's third headmaster as the first era of Kent's hundred year history came to an end after Father Sill suffered a series of strokes.

In the fall of 1941, Kent began its year with 35 faculty and 308 students. The average tuition fee was $900, very much in line with Father Sill's earlier estimate that tuition should equal the cost of a mid-size car. But while dark clouds were gathering on the horizon, the School was certainly taken by surprise on December 7, when the Japanese bombed Pearl Harbor. The country was at war.

Left: Wilbur L. Cross, governor of Connecticut, and Franklin D. Roosevelt, governor of New York, with Fr. Sill at a meeting in the town of Kent in 1931.

42

Right: Schoolhouse under construction in 1936.

Below: Schoolhouse labs.

Kent School Grocery Requirements 1931-32

5 boxes of 48 cans Sardines (1 lb. tins)
4   "   100 cans Sardines (3¼ oz. ")
2   "   12 - 2 lb. jars Grape Preserve
3 pails Red Currant Jelly (30 lb. Pails)
1 doz. Chili Sauce (No. 10 tins)
1 keg   Sour Pickles (5 gal.)
1 kit   Prepared Mustard (5 gal. kits)
1 gal. Worcestershire Sauce
1 bbl. Vinegar - dark - 55 gals.
2 doz. Karo Syrup - Blue Ribbon - 10 lb. cans
10 lbs. Shredded Cocoanut
1 case Bulk Chocolate (10 lb. cakes)
25 bls. Granulated Gelatine
25 lbs. Pearl Tapioca
4 boxes Thompsons Small Seedless Raisins - 25 lb. boxes
1   "   Baker's Seedless Raisins - 30 lb.
1   "   Drained Citron - 10 lb.
4   "   Dried Apricots - 25 lb.
2   "   Black Figs - 25 lbs.
40   "   Prunes - 60/70 or 50/60 size - 25 lb.
6   "   Kelloggs Corn Flakes - 10 lb. bulk
1 case Kelloggs Corn Flakes - 19-lb. 36- 8 oz. pkts.
8 cartons Quaker Puffed Rice - 18 - 4½ oz. pkts.
8   "   Quaker Puffed Wheat - 18 - 4 oz.
8 cases Kelloggs Shredded Wheat - 24 - 12½ oz.
4 cases Quaker Crackels (18 - 7 oz.)
6 cases Malt Breakfast Food (12- 1 3/8 lb.)
6   "   Ralston Breakfast Food (18 - 1½ lb.)
6   "   Wheatena -(18 - 1 3/8 lb.)
10 boxes Macaroni (20 lb. bulk)
2 bags State White Pea Beans (100 lbs)
1   "   New Calif. Dried Lima Beans (100 lbs)
1   "   Black Turtle Beans (100 lb. bags)
2   "   Fancy Head Rice (100 lb. bags)
2   "   Yellow Corn Meal (100 lb. bag)
2   "   Corn Starch (50 lb. bags)
1 cart. Domino Sugar Tablets (60 lb Cartons - 2 lb. each)
2 bbls. Table Salt (280 lb. barrels)
10 bags Ice Cream Salt (100 lb. bags)
6 lbs. Ground Cinnamon (6 lb box)
3   "   Whole Cloves
6   "   Black Pepper Ground
6   "   Paprika

Above: Kent School's shopping list in the early '30s.
Left: Razing North Building.

Even without the war, it would have been difficult for Fr. Chalmers, who had been acting as headmaster since Father Sill's first stroke in 1939. Imagine trying to step into the shoes of a legend while that legend was alive and living at the School. And when one considers what that first year of his headship brought, the fact that he brought the school safely through turbulent times becomes even more remarkable. Six months after Father Chalmers became headmaster, the United States was at war, and many of Kent's young men were

Miss Florence Sill

In any history of the early years at Kent, Miss Florence Sill, Father Sill's sister, deserves mention, for it was she who was given the task of keeping the boys happy. She came to Kent in 1936, and her first job, apparently, was to clean up the third floor of the Dining Hall so that she could move in. According to a vignette in the *Kent News*, her life "was one merry-go-round of teas for the boys." Born in New York, she graduated from Barnard with the Class of 1900 and decided upon a literary career. "But the Church intervened and soon she was conducting a Bible and sewing school." After teaching at a girls' school for six years, Miss Sill came to Kent where she became a tradition. "Since her arrival here, Florence Miller Sill has become rather a tradition. Her teas are the most glorious to be had; her parties for her Dining Hall tables are more reminiscent of days gone by than anything else that ever happens about the place. In her first days, Pater told Miss Sill to try to keep the boys happy. From the start this has been her aim, and it has paid dividends to us all" (*Kent News*).

on their way to Europe, North Africa, and the Pacific, some of them never to return. Rationing brought physical hardships to the school—though the farm made life less difficult than it might otherwise have been. However, life at Kent continued, and as in the Depression, the principles on which Kent was founded—Simplicity of Life, Self-reliance, and Directness of Purpose—kept the School on a steady course.

"By any measure it had to have been difficult for Fr. Chalmers to lead Kent School as the successor of the zealous founder and strong administrator that Fredrick Herbert Sill, OHC—'Pater'—had been, especially since the stern figurehead of Kent was still there exerting a powerful influence on the valley, albeit with greatly lessened capacities and diminished in energy as the result of a massive stroke in 1946. Still, Fr. Sill's white robe and large black cross hanging around his neck provided an imposing figure, even as he sat in his wheelchair to watch students at lunch in the Dining Hall and going to class and going to chapel and playing in sports, uttering directives and pointed questions in his slurred speech for everyone, and everyone knew who he was and what Kent meant to him as well as what he had meant to Kent. Though he could not speak plainly and his energy flagged, he could exert his will in its critical fashion. And he was always there, watching, watching the activities, the schedules and the directions of the school.

"Like any new venture, it was difficult to build up the financial support necessary to make Kent School strong. As a non-profit, sliding-scale educational institution, it was all the more difficult. With the passing of the torch from Pater, the founder, to a successor-administrator, the financial footing of Kent School was soft and tremulous at best. The situation did not improve in the time that Fr. Chalmers was there, for whatever reason. As a fellow member of the Order of the Holy Cross, Fr. Chalmers was personally close to Pater, bound

CLIFTON K. LOOMIS

Clifton K. Loomis was a forthright man. When he approved, he absolutely exploded with approval. His disapproval, similarly, was no subtle implication, and it was never sarcastic. Sometimes he hurled inattentive or ill-prepared creatures in the flesh through the doorway of his classroom, and hurled their books and papers out into the hall after them. I remember his glittering at one of my contemporaries—a

Clifton K. Loomis.

man since of considerable public note—and barking, "I don't like you, (so and so), and I doubt that I ever do. But I plan to do my damndest to make something of you!" When I mentioned this to Clif years later, he still didn't like so and so.

Mr. Loomis was a great English teacher, a great Anglican church man, a great admirer of good prose and poetry, particularly of the aged-in-the-wood sort. (He savored Browning). He was also, by devout avocation, a Vermont dairy farmer, and, as I found out later, a fermenter of excellent hard cider and a mixer of dreadful martinis.

When I first saw him, Clif was in his early fifties, a big bald man whose limbs, torso, and pace assured the world that it would take dynamite to move him where he chose not to go. In the thirty years of our friendship, he changed hardly at all in these or in other respects. Boys in class watched his gleaming and resolute face with extreme caution. Very hard of hearing and festooned with boxes and wires which worked only fairly well, Clif parlayed the handicap into about the only teaching aid he ever used. To answer his questions required a serious turning up of volume as well as clear enunciation. He was firm on the subject: what he did not hear was a wrong answer; so not many of his students turned out mumblers. Furthermore, since there is a considerable difference for self-respecting people between murmuring

nonsense and shouting it, the majority of Clif's pupils came prepared.

Clif was not much interested in teaching descriptive grammar as theory, but intensely concerned with correct usage. He liked imaginative writing and controlled flourishes of style on our papers. Boys who were not up to fresh phrasing or allusive expression he might like and even admire, if their papers were clear and correct, but he rolled out his real encomia for those who regularly had some unusual notions couched in Johnsonian or Chesterfieldian prose.

He extolled, admired, and assigned Dr. Johnson, and like Johnson, Mr. Loomis was in many respects a man who had made up his mind. Since his mind was remarkably well-stocked, this quality did not generally result in narrow views or intolerance, but it did make us careful to have solid grounds for our occasional dissents. We were left in no doubt as to what we were dissenting from.

THE REVEREND WILLIAM C. WOODS

The Reverend William C. Woods, Ph.D., was head of the science department. He sometimes referred to himself as Blueberry Bill, but was known and addressed as Pop. Pop's most striking superficial characteristic was his high soft voice. Along with Father Sill he was one of the two most easily mimicked people I have ever met. (Come to think of it, though, Clif's bark, punctuated by mighty throat clearings wasn't hard to take off either). Pop's knowledge and intellect, on the other hand, defied accurate imitation. He was an extraordinarily learned man, not only in his immediate professional fields of chemistry, biology, and theology. He subscribed to a lending library which sent him ponderous weekly shipments of current books on all sorts of subjects

(continued)

and in a bewildering array of genres. He was as widely read in literature and history as many members of the departments staking official claim to those areas. All this, of course, I found out well after my schooldays. For Kent School students his bibliomania and resulting catholicity of reference appeared obliquely as part of a private subtle jest he played on them. His role for them was that of the Simple Soul, a timid unsophisticated recluse

The Reverend William C. Woods, Ph.D.

who was ingenuously impressed by the athletic prowess he had never had, and ever ready to reward touchdowns with high biology grades. As I learned later, he had only a modest interest in boys' games, and he had a highly sophisticated skepticism about marks and marking systems in general and in their local versions. Because he liked his students, he watched them play, and because he could trick them into working well by doing so, he pretended to be whimsically sentimental at grading. When I did tumble to this charade and taxed him with it, he observed mildly, "Teaching is a ruthless business."

People did get very good marks in biology from Pop. When he silkily assured me, for example, that my 93.5 was entirely due to winning wrestling matches, I am not sure whether or not I really believed him in my heart. Believing him publicly, however, was a social duty of the time and place. College board scores and later work in college confirmed that he had either taught or conned me into a knowledge of elementary biology worth, roughly, 93.5.

Frank V. Anders.

Father Woods was rector of St. Andrew's Parish, Kent. Except on an ocean picnic in Maine some time during the '50's, I never saw Pop otherwise dressed than in dusty, rusty, black clericals.

FRANK V. ANDERS

Somewhere between the physical thunder of Mr. Loomis's classroom personality and the Florentine guile of Father Woods's are my memories of Mr. Frank V. Anders, head of mathematics and physics. He was known as Deac, and we boys believed that he was or had been a deacon in the Episcopal Church. He did not practice ecclesiastically in the chapel, nor was there any other evidence beyond his customary sober garb and demeanor to support the legend of ordination. He did, however, perform one armed chin-ups on the door frame of his classroom. Perhaps he did so to demonstrate some principle of physics which I have either forgotten or never took in, but as a demonstration, gravely executed, the feat kept the class's attention on the man. That was partly due to the fascinating power that mystery had for us. Deac was of particularly formal and impassive appearance, a grave, slender man who seemed to us somehow to have been born in his late middle age and to have lingered there permanently. Deac's speaking voice was dry and precise, a voice which might have been lacking in appeal if it were not for his practice of saying rather raffish things with it. "Watch'em Kent. Go get 'em," he would grate out as we pursued blackboard problems in geometry. Our popular wisdom held that Deac knew everything about math and that he could solve all problems of quantity devised by man or machine. That faith was verified by our certainty that Deac had infallible powers over what stocks and bonds were sure to do. Our unassailable legend was that he had conquered where so many had fallen during the depression and that he continued to make daily killings on the Stock Market. Just why such a talent should postulate mathematical genius our innocence did not choose to entertain. I learned years later from Clif Loomis that Deac had indeed given him some valuable tips for investment, but mere evidence is but a trifle here. As his students we did not want the facts as to whether or not Deac was really a deacon, a mathematical wizard, a physical phenomenon, or a Wall Street conquistador. Those things were enigmatical laws of local nature. Excellent teacher that he was, Deac was to us a formidable mystery, and that is how we wanted him to continue.

Along with the differences implied or noted in these bare sketches, the three past masters had certain professional qualities in common which were not entirely personal but in some measure imposed by the times and circumstances they shared at Kent. Their function was all but entirely pedagogical; they were teachers, master teachers. Father Sill was not himself terribly interested in the offerings of classroom or study hall, but he knew that somebody had to be if his school was to be in fact a school. So he made sure that in every important area of the curriculum he had at least one long-term senior man who was absolutely absorbed in his subject and who had proven credentials as a superior practitioner of its instruction. In a strange sense, he set up such men as Loomis, Woods, and Anders as his internal adversaries up to a point, of course. Thus, if the Old Man felt the urge to pull everyone out of class or study to sweep hockey rinks or to enjoy a three-hour disciplinary job assembly, he knew that he had solid disapproval before him. Not that he would necessarily be deterred, but he felt some restraint all the same.

—O.B. Davis

in the protocol of the Order with Pater who was still the definite senior Kent partner. Then again, the reason might well have laid in the nature of people (investors) who wait to see if an institution can survive the passing power of the founder who was still overseeing events. Fr. Chalmers had to be strong, but not too strong" (Michael West).

Not only did Father Chalmers face the inevitable stresses inherent in being the headmaster of a great boarding school, he also faced the special stresses of doing this in a country at war on two fronts. In the fall of 1942, the US government changed the Selective Service Act to permit the drafting of 18-year-old boys and outlawing college for all, except in a few cases in which students might be prepared for specialized training or would be totally unprepared to do anything but carry a gun. In addition to creating a summer school so that students could complete their Kent education, the School made changes in its curriculum to cope with the draft, trying "to arrange the schedule of each boy so that he will complete his course and have the necessary fifteen points for graduation and college entrance before he reaches his eighteenth

Below: Fr. Sill on the occasion of the 32nd anniversary of the founding of Kent School, 1938.

March 1, 1941.

I am very happy. The meeting of the Alumni Council, to be called now Alumni Trustees, on the night of February 21st, with the four Trustees of the Kent School Corporation, resulted in the election of the Reverend William Scott Chalmers, O. H. C., as the next Headmaster of Kent School, his election to be announced on Prize Day. I am to be retired. The Father Superior of the Order, who is Chairman of our Trustees, accepted my resignation and immediately nominated Father Chalmers. The Alumni Trustees had already expressed their hearty approval of this step.

This is all I will say for the present. I ask all friends of Kent School to consider this as expressing my own personal approval of this step and I will look forward with pleasure to serving the School to the best of my capacity.

This is an informal announcement and does not take the place of the Father Superior's formal announcement on Prize Day. I want to thank all the Alumni for their hearty cooperation in this historic move towards the future of Kent.

Above: Father Sill announced his retirement and the appointment of Fr. Chalmers to succeed him.

Below: The Reverend William Scott Chalmers, O.H.C., the third headmaster of Kent School.

birthday" (*Kent News*, February 3, 1943). Many sixth formers left to enter military service, and the school had to make up for their departure by increasing the size of the underforms. Other aspects of wartime added to the complicated job of running a school. Food rationing meant that each student had to bring his ration book to school so that those foodstuffs being rationed could be purchased. The amount of meat, butter, etc., that could be purchased for each person was limited by the government. Even the athletic schedule was affected, as gasoline rationing curtailed the fall football schedule, limiting contests to those schools that could reach each other by train.

A possibly unexpected change occurred in the 1943-1944 academic year. First, Henry Russell '26 became the first layman elected to the Kent School Board of Trustees. Until then all trustees had been members of the Order of the Holy Cross. Then on May 3, 1945, Father Chalmers announced at the Fathers' Association meeting that the Order had decided that it could no longer take sole responsibility for the School. Because of that decision, Father Chalmers withdrew from the Order so that he could continue at Kent. He then transferred to the Oratory of the Good Shepherd.

The spring of 1945 was momentous in other ways, too. On April 12, 1945, the nation was shocked to hear that Franklin Delano Roosevelt had died in Warm Springs, Georgia, where he was resting. Only a month later, grief turned to joy when, on May 8, 1945, Germany capitulated and there was victory in Europe. Three months later, on August 14, 1945, Japan surrendered, ending World War II.

In his speech to the annual alumni dinner in New York, celebrating Pater's 75th birthday in 1949, Father Chalmer's commented on the challenges and triumphs of those years.

"[L]et me sketch the outstanding events of the last nine years for they tell their own story of the strength of Kent, and all who have had responsibility for it. Almost immediately upon my accession as headmaster our country was plunged into war. This, together with the inevitable problems related to the transition from one headmaster to another, and further complicated by the decision of the Order of the Holy Cross to withdraw from its responsibility for the School, made the years until 1946 quite unusual. These last two years have seen the School coping with the problems presented by the inflationary conditions of the post-war period and the unusually competitive situation in regard to college entrance.

"Kent has emerged from this series of crises and challenges with its essential spirit intact and in good shape to enter upon the next step in its development."

Father Chalmers went on to point out that the debt on the Library building had been paid and that the New Main Building, "the final unit in the permanent fire-proof plant," had been built. Masters were being paid competitive salaries, and the intellectual life of the school was steadily improving.

William Scott Chalmers, third headmaster of Kent, announced his resignation in March of 1949, stating:

> While the days of the wooden buildings and the coal furnaces are gone, and with them a certain ruggedness and simplicity of life you all appreciated (at least in retrospect), these challenges have been replaced by others equally fruitful for the boys now at Kent. Just as I doubt whether I could now qualify for entrance to the University I attended in the '20's, I doubt if some of you could qualify for the standard of studies now prevailing at Kent. It is impossible for me to speak with the same objectivity of the spiritual life at Kent during this period. That is what concerns me most directly. It is where I am most conscious of repeated failures. The response of the boys while they are at School and after leaving makes me grateful, indeed. Their lack of response causes heart searchings.
>
> Having said all this I must also say that these nine years when I have had responsibility for the leadership of Kent have been a time of transition. Kent has been moving from the small school of the earlier years to the established institution of the present and the future. It is my belief and prayer this change has been taking place both with due regard to its cherished traditions and ideals, and with awareness of its increased responsibilities to boys who are to enter the world of today and tomorrow. Now this change needs to be recognized in the organization of the school. If the boys are to continue to receive the spiritual food, the intellectual stimulus, the impetus to self-reliance and the healthy recreation we covet for them there must be a re-arrangement of responsibility.

The Kent News of April 6, 1949, responded to the news of Father Chalmers's announcement in an editorial.

> Chief came to Kent in 1939 as priest and assistant to Father Sill. When Pater was forced to resign due to his illness, Father Chalmers took over his job as headmaster, a position which he

KENT ALUMNI KILLED IN THE SERVICE OF THEIR COUNTRY IN THE SECOND WORLD WAR

Frederick Howden '21

Wallace Trapnell '21

David Harmon '27

Andrew Hero '27

George Robertson '29

William Gillespie '30

John Gott '32

Orson Hammond '32

Dunstan Perkins '32

H. Melvin Young '32

John Runnalls '33

Andrew Lawson-Tancred '33
(an ESU student)

Lindgren Bancroft '34

Walton Rodgers '34

Arthur Derby '35

Alton Greeley '35

William Coleman Jr. '36

Jesse Davis '36

R. Mulford Jordan Jr. '36

Auville Eager ' 37

Cruger Edgerton '37 MIA

William Harris '37

F. Homer Tate '37

William Aycrigg '38

William Briggs '38

Jonathan Bullard '38

H. Victor Crawford '38

William Jackson '38

Hambleton Symington '38

John Bergamini Jr. '39

Harold Connett Jr. '39

William Schmidt Jr. '39

Theodore Sterling Jr. '39

Augustus Van Cortland 3rd '39

Gardner Anstice '40

Norman Conze '40

Sandwith Drinker '40

Charles Jones '40

John Dryden '41

Adrian Tapscott '41

David Stimson '44

Robert Pogue '44

The World War II Memorial Plaque in St. Joseph's Chapel.

has faithfully fulfilled ever since.

From the beginning, Father Chalmers realized that taking the place of as great a man as Pater would not be easy, but he did his job willingly and with much interest in the welfare of the School. Since his arrival, the School has continued to progress under its original ideals of simplicity of life, directness of purpose, and self-reliance. In 1946 the Permanent Kent of Pater's dreams was at last realized when the New Main Building was completed, thus ending a period of growth and expansion which has resulted in the Kent of today.

Until the present time the school has been building itself up into one of the country's finest. It must now enter a new phase in its history. Kent must now strive to preserve all that it has stood for and become over the years, for getting on top and staying on top are equally difficult. If everyone associated with Kent does a sincere and faithful a job in helping preserve Pater's ideals as has Father Chalmers, the School will always maintain its principles of simplicity of life, directness of purpose, and self-reliance.

After leaving Kent, Father Chalmers became the headmaster of Harvard School, the college preparatory school of the Episcopal Diocese of Los Angeles in North Hollywood, where he enjoyed great success. His twenty years there are referred to as the Chalmers years in the official history of the school, and the Upper School building was named Chalmers Hall in his honor. During his time as headmaster he was awarded a special citation by the City of Los Angeles and a Doctorate of Divinity from Occidental College. He was also president of the board of trustees of the Dunn School. During the last eleven years of his life he was actively associated with St. Mark's-in-the-Valley Episcopal Church in Solvang, California, as assisting priest and chairman of the new church building committee. At St. Mark's a chapel named in his honor serves as a permanent memorial to Father Chalmers.

Father Chalmers was succeeded as headmaster by the Reverend John Oliver Patterson on November 1, 1949. The student body numbered 310 boys. A young man named Otis Benson Davis '42 began his career teaching English. Soccer became a regular fall sport. German, which hadn't been taught since before World War II, returned to the curriculum, and Greek, which hadn't been taught since 1945, was again offered to fifth and sixth formers. Kent was ready to move into the post-war world of the 1950s.

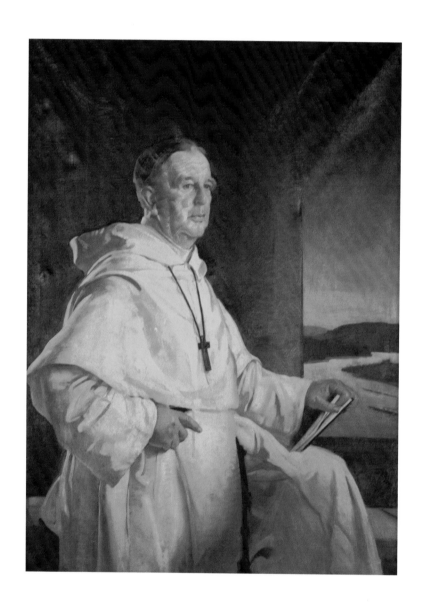

THE REVEREND FREDERICK HERBERT SILL, OHC

1874–1952

On July 17, 1952, Father Patterson wrote to the alumni and friends of Kent to tell them that Father Sill had died.

To the Alumni and Friends of Kent:

With the same great faith that has always marked his spirit and his work, Father Sill died peacefully today, July 17, 1952.

Although his strength failed rapidly during the past month, he seemed to suffer no distress and was able to receive the Blessed Sacrament shortly before his death.

Burial will be at St. Joseph's Chapel at 11:00 A.M. on July 21ˢᵗ and there will be a memorial service at Trinity Church, Wall Street, New York at 11:00 A.M. on Thursday, July 24ᵗʰ.

Pater will always be remembered with great love and loyalty and respect by all who knew him. He has built a monument in Kent School that we pray will always command and merit that same love and loyalty and respect.

May he rest in peace and may light perpetual shine upon him.

Sincerely,

John O. Patterson

It was clear that Kent's Founder had made an impression on the world, not simply on the valleyland of Kent and the Kent Family. On July 21, an editorial in The New York Herald Tribune *headed "Father Sill of Kent" celebrated his life.*

Men when they die leave various achievements behind them to stand as their memorials. The Rev. Dr. Frederick Herbert Sill, who has died at seventy-eight, leaves behind him a truly living memorial— a school. Father Sill founded Kent School on the Housatonic River in Connecticut in 1906. Its first quarters were in a farmhouse, its first faculty consisted of three masters, its first student body numbered eighteen. Today Kent's physical establishment is valued at $1,500,000 and it is invariably ranked as one of American's foremost boys' schools. Yet one feature of that first semester in 1906 continues unchanged to these days. Kent boys did their own chores then, and they do them now. For at Kent education includes an understanding of the eminently valuable art of sweeping the floor.

No school reflects the personality and characteristics of its founder better than Kent School reflects Father Sill's. In its devotion to religion, to self-dependence, to the highest ideals of scholarship, it bears his mark indelibly. Even its prowess in crew racing stems directly from Father Sill, for, as a young man, he was coxswain of the Columbia College crew, which he led to victory in the first Poughkeepsie Regatta ever held. Although he suffered a paralytic stroke and retired from active work in 1941, Father Sill remained at his home on the school grounds, watching over the changing generations of youth, and pecking out letters on a typewriter to the countless Kent alumni who loved to hear from him. His name endures in their hearts, as it does in the school to which he devoted his life.

The Herald Tribune *reported on Father Sill's funeral in its July 22, 1952 issue, reporting that nearly 500 persons filled the chapel to overflowing. "As the chapel was filling, a band of bell ringers composed of alumni and undergraduates rang Grandsire Doubles on half-muffled bells in the chapel tower and the sound carried through the muggy air of this Housatonic Valley town. In the chapel stalls ten members of the Order of the Holy Cross, in their white woolen habits, began intoning centuries-old plainsong chants. . . . After the mass, the coffin [a plain wooden one made by the school carpenter] was carried to the chapel garden and placed in the grave marked by a simple oaken cross. . . . Then, one by one, members of the Order of the Holy Cross and the pallbearers sprinkled the grave with holy water. In the tower, the ton-and-a-half tenor bell tolled seventy-eight times, a stroke for each of Father Sill's years."*

In Time, *July 28, 1952, Father Sill's life was celebrated. The article began with the story of a "famous function—the night the headmaster sat in for a sick violinist at [Kent's] dance. The Reverend Frederick Herbert Sill, priest of the Protestant Episcopal Order of the Holy Cross, fiddled till midnight so that his boys and their girls could dance to proper music. From the raised band platform he could also keep an eye on student manners. Any Kent boy who departed from propriety got a smart rap with the master's fiddle bow as he danced by.*

"Few of the boys were surprised at Father Sill's versatility. At Kent they were ready to believe that the restless little cleric could do anything. He was the school's founder, . . .; he presided over the discipline of the school, taught religion and English, supervised admissions; he coached football, hockey and crew; he acted as chaplain, purchasing agent, business manager and dietician. For his boys, Father Sill prescribed his precepts of hard work and simple faith. . . . And under Headmaster Sill's uncompromising leadership, in 46 years Kent has taken its place high up in the ranks of Eastern preparatory schools."

FHS
A FAITH THAT DID NOT FAIL

WHEN PATER DIED, AFTER SUPPORTING SO COURAGEOUSLY his cruel illness of years, not a few Kent men of the early classes must have said to themselves: there's the end of Kent School. Grounds for the sad surmise were not far to find. With the hand that shaped Kent no longer able to guide, or active to care for Kent, signs of change began very soon to appear; and those who knew the earlier school had watched for some time with uneasiness—an uneasiness all the greater because one could not really say what was happening; one could only ask. The difference, the change, had been not so much seen as felt.

Seen changes, changes of form, are those that time unfailingly exacts; they are part of any continuing life; and they are often requisite. Doing things differently may be a lasting institution's very means of remaining what it was. The change unseen, the change only felt, is usually another matter. That kind of change goes to spirit, or at least, attitude; and here what may be true of changed form cannot be true. Change here is no saving adjustment to new days and different conditions. Change here is a lethal change of alteration by abandonment. If it proceeded, such a change must mean a different school—no longer Kent.

There had been then, the disturbing perceptible fact of changes felt, the signs of slow changing. If this could have happened with Pater living still, still present at Kent, must not those signs be portents? What could they mean but that Kent had been the projection of one man's vital personality? One resolute mind conceived Kent. Overcoming every obstacle, one man's unique vigor created it. One strong heart warmed it with life. That vigor gone, the school was showing

a want of sustenance. Though appearances were left, though a school of sorts that bore the name and used the buildings could profess for awhile to be the same school, when that heart stilled, must not the already shortening day of the real Kent be done?

To affirm just that, recollection and reflection joined quickly. Kent had been Kent because Pater had been Pater. The interdependence was impressive. What was meant by Kent could not be found in any assemblage of buildings, in any faculty and student body. Kent meant that carriage of the head, majestic and leonine; the sharp-eyed turn of the forceful face, softening to smile or alert to frown; the vigorous movement of the sloping but strong shoulders from which the coarse white habit, majestic, too, took its energetic swing. Kent also meant, the majestic being put off, that different affectionately-to-be-remembered costume, for convenience in coaching sports put on in its various variations—those deplorable knickerbockers; that sweater; that used baseball cap, or the winter thing of wool that could be pulled down! Did ever another headmaster walk with dignity so indefeasible that no fear for dignity, no thought for mere appearance, need enter his head—or, on the same point, was there ever another headmaster whose sufficient setting was of so little state as the old study—hardly more than a made-over attic? Kent meant also that unfashionable apartment; sloped walls covered with shabby matchboard, each vertical wall, before, behind, and out to the dormer windows, jammed frame to frame with photographs in no order or arrangement; carpeted with that very wreck of a rug; over-supplied with any-old furniture battered and scuffed by many school generations of sixth-formers taking tea and other formers taking sacred studies; and, for the proprietor's own relaxation, that sagged easychair beside the desk to which he could move when

---

First printed in 1956 for the 50th Anniversary celebration.

not at work, settling with formidable lack of grace and a magisterial but good-natured glancing through his horn-rimmed glasses while he filled from the pound tin of Prince Albert tobacco his wholly utilitarian bulldog pipe.

Such affecting reminiscence can and did easily lead—we shall not look upon his like again!-- to conclusions of seeming moral certainty. To a same conclusion tended arguments perhaps more logical; drier facts. Why was the concept of Kent proving, as slowly but surely it appeared to be, incommunicable? On the face, neither obscure, nor complicated, nor even highly individual, the concept looked easy to grasp. No definition could have been plainer: this was a school which would especially encourage simplicity of life, self-reliance, and directness of purpose. In so plain a statement of ends, an equally plain statement of means, a rule or measure, seemed implicit. Anything that offered this encouragement belonged at Kent; anything that didn't, didn't.

In Pater's Kent the concept was always grasped easily. There, as well as implicit, the enabling means were explicit. Questions to perplex—exactly what do we mean by simplicity of life, by self-reliance, by directness of purpose? Exactly how do you encourage them?--had not been anticipated because in Pater's day they never could have arisen. They did not arise because Pater's Kent knew without question what was meant by those terms. Simplicity of life was Pater's everyday way of living. Self-reliance was Pater's competent and capable practice of doing things for himself when a man could dig if he tried; to beg, he should indeed be ashamed! Directness of purpose was Pater's own honesty of intention, an integrity of unskimped effort that had no truck with vain show or false pretence. As for what encouragement consisted in, what else but the obvious measures by which doing things they ought to do in realization of Kent's objectives was made easy for boys, while doing things they ought not to do was made hard? That these measures were to him never anything but obvious was Pater's gift—approaching, in fact, genius. Where the Kent he meant to make, and made, was concerned, he was given to know with

intuitive certainty, with instant unreflecting sureness, what was, whatever the situation, the required measure, the one right thing to do next.

This kind of knowledge, the intuition that is genius, is never to be gained by taking thought. Study and experience may get a man information; by themselves, they do not get him understanding. Where the rare insight called understanding comes from isn't easily said. That loving is involved seems probable; yet the evidences of life suggest that loving is a consequence, not a cause. The real source often seems to be in a power of imagination by which the man who is inspired to understand not only transposes himself, puts himself in another's place; but, momentarily, for the purposes of the enlightening moment, virtually *becomes* the other. Looking back, one guesses this to have been Pater's gift. Not losing nor impairing the man's judgment, and with none of the unnaturalness of most grown-ups who, ill-advised, (fooling no boy) offer to act the boy, he could at will and need become the boy. He felt the feelings of a boy. He could accept as real the values of a boy. A boy's wants were obvious to him; a boy's intentions were readily foreseeable.

The result was that when the undeliberated magical transposition took place in Pater, the boy in any boy, whether he was able to realize (he probably wouldn't be) what was happening or not, recognized the real thing. The mature man still confronted him; but present in the man had come to be someone who thought understandable thoughts and talked comprehensible language. On the one hand, an alliance of interest became perfectly feasible. If a boy needed help in doing those things that he ought to do, an uncondescending auxiliary, a trusty comrade, stood reassuringly ready to go, with a grown man's dazzling resources, with patience and kindness, to all trouble to help him help himself. On the other hand—and quite as important—that mysterious familiar who spoke as a boy, understood as a boy, thought as a boy, was (for that very reason) not easy for a boy to hoodwink. You would be unwise to tell him the sort of lie adults usually swallowed. Knowing what to look for, he readily found out wrongdoing, easily identified mischief, and moved, often memorably, to discourage them. In themselves, as abstractions, patience and long-suffering may always be good; in practice, and particularly in this practice, whose subject is the unlicked cub, the callow youth, in his half-learning still mainly oaf and fool, mildness may be no kindness. Measures too temperate do boys the disservice of misleading them about a life in which you reap what you sow, and of misleading them—by letting them think they deserve to be indulged when they don't—about themselves. How wholesome the qualms of consternation, how salutary the examinings of conscience, with which many of us once started when we heard that anxious word passed: *the Old Man's on a rampage!* Whether in disciplining one contumacious brat, or rating the whole school for some momentary idleness or refractoriness, the wisdom of instinct made how few mistakes, failed how seldom justly to determine, each in due season, the time for helping, the time for chastising, the time for forgiving!

The argument of despond had been, of course, that these remembered things, all meaning Kent, and so many of them highly personal, so many of them quite inimitable, must add up to Kent. Yet, did they? In the count of arresting qualities, in the recollection of that particular genius, was something overlooked, something left out? The effective approving kindnesses, the effective measures of disapproval, were, in essence, works; what of faith? What had been Pater's life and work—they were really one—but a long act of faith? His faith had been that he would find ways, that means would discover themselves, to accomplish every purpose of good. Practice of this faith, with the experience of faith so often rewarded, could be observed to have formed in Pater, as years passed, a sustaining confidence, a clear conviction. If he, with the love that was easy, with the patience that sometimes came hard, did his part, his best, bread cast upon the waters would be found. The conviction was not the satisfied pride of a man who sees rightly that he has done what many men couldn't have done. That part of the conclusion of despond that proved personal regard, that told him how much he was missed, would no doubt have touched him; but one can guess the

almost irate objection he surely would have offered—what? Could there be, among those he had taught to know better, so blank a misunderstanding of what he aimed at; what he worked for; what, by grace, he had in fact accomplished?

In words of another noted headmaster, to which Pater recurred often enough to show how full of meaning he found them: he strove for success, without ever thinking himself successful. The humility of an instructed mind—one well aware of how much must always be left to do—would not rest on what was already done, nor bother to sum up preliminary gains. Not in Pater would it be to figure Kent School as a personal triumph—Kent, as his. Rather, with humble confidence, with religious certainty, he was Kent's—the concept's instrument, its implement. His own whole life of hard glad service, the ceaseless demanding use Kent had made of him, assured him of that concept's power. Would he ever have desponded over temporary difficulties or little delays?

Nothing, we may be sure, shook his faith. His faith was that the spirit of that purpose which had found and used him so well would, in its own time and way find others fit to use. Others would grasp it, cherish it; and so, with an aroused resource, with devotion like his own, gladly serve. They would serve as he had served—not in mechanical rehearsings of any past; but in creative renewing, the free recreating which on each new day and each new tomorrow could provide (as he had always provided) the means and forms to keep Kent, Kent. Its author and its instrument, could Pater ever have doubted—should anyone have doubted?--that the superintendent spirit lived, which, living, informing, guiding, only waiting to draw to it its own, would take care that what was Kent's would know Kent's face?

—James Gould Cozzens '22

III
A Nucleus of Virtues

THE MAN CHOSEN TO CONTINUE THE WORK BEGUN BY FATHER SILL AND continued by Father Chalmers was another Episcopal priest, the Reverend John Oliver Patterson, the rector of Grace Church, Madison, Wisconsin. In 1946, Father Patterson, along with Massey Shepherd, Samuel E. West, and John H. Keene, had founded the Associated Parishes for Liturgy and Mission. These four priests used their own parishes as laboratories for the new liturgical movement in the Episcopal Church. Much of what we take for granted today in the Episcopal Church is the result of their vision: the Eucharist as the main service on Sundays, the offertory procession in which the bread and wine are brought to the altar, the gospel procession that brings the reading of the gospel into the congregation, and "music that all could sing." Marriages, baptisms, and funerals became public events. The changes extended to parish life, also, with committees established to take care of such things as stewardship, education, and buildings and grounds. "Associated Parishes also sought to forge links between the liturgy and social issues such as racial justice." And finally, by the 1960s, the need for a new prayer book became obvious, and after many trial liturgies, the 1979 *Book of Common Prayer* was passed by the General Convention. All of this grew out of the work of the Reverend John Oliver Patterson and his three associates. (Information from http://polymer.bu.edu/~jdm/ap.html)

Father Patterson arrived at Kent in the fall of 1949, and the thirteen years of his leadership brought the second big phase of Kent's physical and academic development. Michael H. West, son of the Reverend Samuel E. West, Assistant Headmaster and Chaplain from 1949 to 1959, has written extensively about Father Patterson. Selections from his essay "Kent of the Fifties," supplemented with selections from Father Patterson's own writings (in italics), follow.

"John Oliver Patterson was Kent's fourth headmaster. An architect who had entered the priesthood in 1934, a parish priest with a wife and children rather than the member of an order, Father Patterson came from Grace Church, Madison, Wisconsin, with Raydon P. Ronshaugen and The Reverend Samuel West to lead Kent after a somewhat difficult transition from the disabled founder to a headmaster who lived under the imposing shadow of the founder."

*Above: The Reverend John Oliver
Patterson in 1955.*

I can state my goal for Kent quite briefly—that it be without question the finest possible Christian School. Our aim is to turn out not merely educated men, but educated Christian men—men who can find real stature in this universe.

I am quite aware that ideals without specific techniques for their expression can quickly degenerate into sentimentalities. Such a program of Christian education does not grow out of mere good intentions, but requires that academic standards be the highest, curriculum the wisest and teaching the most effective. It also requires that the Chapel be in the truest sense possible the center of all life on the Campus and that its influence permeate all the study, work and play of the School.

"Father Patterson could be a fascinating man, at once exasperating then inspiring, distant then brilliant, shy and bold all at the same time, hard and humorless, soft and laughing with his whole being, a spiritual man and a practical man, a non-athlete who knew the value of good and great athletes to *esprit de corps*. He was a man nearly always dressed in black who drove a black '57 Chevy convertible with bright tomato-red interior that is still the envy of anyone that knows a flash car.

"Still, to see the legacy, one must look at the great changes that have taken place in one hundred years, and that part of them that came about in the relatively short span of thirteen years surrounding the fifty-year mark of Kent School. What occurred under Father Patterson led to all the changes since, every bit as much as Father Sill's founding of the school changed the Schaghticoke wilderness in 1906."

This has not happened accidentally. Kent School has been built on the strongest faith, the soundest thinking, the highest loyalty. These have resulted in a community with firm traditions, established techniques and carefully planned organization . . . And just so the Kent Way must never be an end in itself. What we are doing must always be seen as a means to an end, and that end is always to teach boys the nature of their environment so that they can relate that environment to themselves intelligently, courageously and effectively. The Kent Way is not directed merely at creating a good school. It is directed at showing boys God's purpose in life and thus bringing to their lives significance, harmony, and stature. This will continue to be the goal of the Kent of the future and all detailed plans will be directed to this end.

"What kind of man can do and build while maintaining an environment of success for such diverse brilliance as an R.E.K. Rourke, William H. Armstrong, James H. Breasted, Hal Bredburg, O.B. Davis, Jake McCandless and on and on, with such differing professional temperaments and personal needs? Brilliant students were no less demanding for attention for their special talents. Students' parents, meanwhile, represented another clientele because the parents held differing reasons for sending and keeping their sons (and, later, daughters) at Kent.

"People who had worked closely with Father Patterson could see different

JAMES PATTON HUMPHREYS

Not long before March 3, Jim Humphreys wrote that he had given up his giant tricycle and for exercise was resorting to a pair of floor pedals. With hindsight, anyway, old friends can recognize his signals. (1) Jim was serving notice that his mortal matters were about concluded; (2) at the same time he was till practicing his old time and familiar *mens sana in corpore sano* principle. He was still writing things down and working out what muscles he could. But Jim's old friends, even those considerably his junior, are in number themselves thinning out on the lathe of time, and, as I have already presumed to suggest, my attempt is mostly directed at those many younger heirs and beneficiaries in our Kent audience who missed knowing a remarkable past master.

My credentials for recalling James Patton Humphreys are modest and incomplete. I have been his Latin pupil, later his faculty colleague, his neighbor in the town of Kent, and a family friend. But my first encounter with him was in 1939, when I was in need of rescue, classically speaking, and was hauled half drowned into Jim's lifeboat section of fourth form Latin. By that time Mr. Humphreys, head of the Classics Department, had already served nineteen distinguished years at Kent. He had also fought a war, played a great deal of tennis, coached football and hockey, traveled abroad, founded and directed a successful tutoring school, and skippered all sorts of sailboats. After 1939, he went on, of course, to many other projects and adventures, including twenty more distinguished years of active Kent faculty duty. After retirement from Kent and the death of his wife, Frankie, Jim took his teaching and coaching not on the road but on the salt sea. In a big sailboat for several years he sailed off to Florida, usually with one not necessarily experienced shipmate. In one winter port or another he would live aboard while teaching a term or so at any of a number of private day schools eager for any time he would afford them. In spare moments he worked on his innovative text *Latin Backwards* along with various chronicles and journals the perusal of which may challenge his survivors to longevities like his own. When he was home in the town of Kent he kept busy writing, teaching, showing all ages by

word and example what to do on the tennis court. Through his seventies, he was the local doubles partner of choice, and in his eighties he won senior tournaments.

But anything I know about JPH's life before 1939 is hearsay, most of it from Jim himself. He was good at hearsay; his long term memory was full of range and detail; his candor absolute. In Latin class we heard a good deal about life in the trenches of World War I, about the eccentric celebrities with whom after the armistice he worked in the Paris office of *Stars and Stripes*, about epic athletic adventures and misadventures, about politics and sanitary facilities during the last days of the Roman republic. Such topics he seasoned with familiar puns and other japeries. He affected no scholarly mannerisms in class and by the time our lot had been winnowed down to a sixth form honors section to study the *Aeneid*, youthful arrogance, vanity, and ignorance had some of us daring to wonder what such matters had to do with Vergil and the college boards. JPH, when he sensed impudent stirrings of that sort, observed from the first book of our text *forsan et haec olim memminisse iuvabit*. Since we could translate the line without looking up anything we were reminded at once that we must have learned some Vergil, and very soon recognized too that our magister was right: we would come to rejoice in remembering those things, along with a great deal else that went on in his class. For Jim knew what he was doing. In emulation of an admired forerunner, the crafty Odysseus, he caught our attention with strange tales and anecdotes in such a way that we hardly noticed the long translation assignments which we competitively performed amid reminiscences, jokes, and conversation. While we hardly noticed he was getting into our smug little skulls the language of Vergil as well as its relationships to our own times and places. Although few if any in that class were nearly as bright as we imagined ourselves to be, those who went on to college Latin found that our sight readings passed for prepared construings, and we could have prospered without cracking a book before class. In occasional emergencies I for one took advantage of that condition, but fortunately for our characters, Jim, along with other benefits bestowed, had given us the habit of doing our homework.

—O.B. Davis

EDMUND FULLER AT KENT SCHOOL

The late John Oliver Patterson, fourth Headmaster of Kent School, recruited Edmund Fuller to Kent's faculty in 1952. The appointment was not controversial, but as Mr. Fuller himself noted, it had some unusual aspects. Edmund had, by 1952, written more than a dozen books, served, as editor-in-chief of Crown Publishers as well as having for some years been in increasing demand as a critic, reviewer, editor, and teacher of post-graduate writing seminars. He was thirty-nine years old, married to a charming lady, father to four talented offspring, and entirely without college or university degrees. In impish moods, he only barely acknowledged having a high school diploma. An autodidact of the very best sort, without the truculent solemnity and self-righteousness sometimes found among the successfully self-educated, Edmund very gladly and swiftly learned and retained all sorts of things and imparted them with wit and with cheer and with not an iota of pomposity.

Edmund Fuller.

Along with a shortage of formal scholastic credentials, Edmund Fuller joined us at Kent as a schoolmaster with a difference in that for the first several years of his tenure he taught no scheduled classes, but instead counted the entire student body as his "section." Remarkably, not to say incredibly, he assigned two books, collateral to English courses, for each of our three hundred and a score of boys. Reading these books and writing a paper on each was the tutorial assignment for everyone, but Mr. Fuller conferred twice during the year with every student, and he read and graded the papers assigned to be appropriate to each conference appointment. I think my recollection accurate as I report that the books involved were not elected by the student body; simply assigned by the Tutor. In any case, though, the tutorial canon from which the readings were drawn reflected Edmund's own reading, and it included many batteries and battalions indeed. Edmund, as I learned as we collaborated in the production of anthologies and other texts, was a lightnin' reader, and a wonderfully comprehending reader, which the majority of so-called "speed readers" are not. It was because he was so fast and so good at understanding language that he was able to operate our impossible and successful tutorial venture.

That he operated it with such adventurous enthusiasm was, in early and mid-fifties anyhow, infectious. Many of the boys caught the infection, a good many to become chronically literate, and nearly all came to take a righteous pride at being treated like adult scholars by this immensely interested and knowledgeable man. And let there be no error about it: although Kent's English department has been habitation to more excellent teachers and scholars than the histories of most good schools can boast, none of our members, past, present, or predicted, can be with confidence cited as Edmund's successful peer at the single-handed running of an all school tutorial. Edmund's work at Kent did not include athletic coaching— he had athletic enthusiasms, but only modest aptitudes for active sport. Playing doubles tennis with him was delightful, but mostly for the wealth of sociability, witty commentary, and general enjoyment he brought to the courts, no matter who the other three fellows were or what on ordinary occasions their skills happened to be. Whatever and wherever the action, and no matter how much muscle and experience it summoned, Edmund was likely to be a lionhearted, if not quite a lionlimbed participant. He was by temperament and code an adventurer. As such he knew well enough the risks life plants for those who move hopefully into new ventures and new places.

—O.B. Davis

aspects of the same person. One was a person who was terribly insecure about his own self-worth. Another was someone bold and abrasive. He was shy and largely uncomfortable with others. He never could be 'one of the boys.' Instead, he pushed ideas into reality, obsessed with the concepts that he worked into bricks and mortar that people walked through in the pursuit of programs for building their personal character and futures in real life.

"He was also a man of great depth of intellectual thought. On the rare occasions that he preached or made guest speeches at other places, it was clear that he thought a great deal about life on earth and in heaven, too. 'Who am I, why am I here and where am I going?' was the opening question to a pointed, terse sermon at St. Joseph's Chapel he made into a speech at Kent Center School on Memorial Day in '56. Who could not relate to such a question of oneself? . . ."

The doctrine of Creation answers the question, "Why are we here?" The doctrine of Grace answers the question, "What are our needs?" It is hard to find any valid motivation for education—or for life—apart from an understanding of God's purpose in creation and it is equally hard to find any effective control of ourselves—or our communities apart from the grace of God. And so it is that the whole future of Kent is devoted to a constantly increasing grasp of God's purpose for man and the means of Grace whereby we can achieve it. Anything less than this is a second-rate goal, unworthy of the label "Christian Education."

"Great courage is the other aspect that lay deep within Father Patterson. He was forever moving forward, sometimes beyond his own abilities and daring, forcing himself to run like hell to forever catch up to his ambitions and promises, which he managed to meet—somehow.

"Once Father Patterson arrived at Kent, in short order the school became strong and hopeful again and started looking to a vastly changing future. Within seven years, by 1956, Kent's 50th anniversary year, the physical plant and academic regimen had changed almost beyond recognition except for the Georgian buildings and the Norman St. Joseph's Chapel that are still in place.

"It was up to Father Patterson to preserve the school within the vision of its mission— excellence in secondary education within the Christian Idea of Education—and build on it, to change it and infuse it with a new energy and excitement. It would require the same self-consuming commitment as the founder had to have had, to preserve something old while bending it into something new to function in the future and to draw future people into sharing the dream of the special greatness that Kent School and its family were and are. He had the vision for the grand scale as well as the eye for small detail, the necessary ingredients for getting things done on the grand scale and the small detail. He and Samuel E. West even changed 'Sacred Studies' to 'Theology,' when he established the Theology Department and a theology course requirement for graduation.

Above: The administration Building seen from the south entrance to St. Joseph's chapel.

"In the thirteen years that he was headmaster, Father Patterson built on all the major aspects of Kent life. Most visible were the changes to the physical plant, making it more efficient and self-contained and building on it to meet the challenges of a higher tech, more competitive future. With energetic Directness of Purpose, he set right to work in the plans to change the face of Kent because he had a limited time frame in which to get things done so that he could build a new foundation for the spiritual and intellectual sides of Kent. The not-so-far-off deadline was 1956, the fiftieth anniversary of the founding of Kent School which would include a year of extraordinary programs, study, evaluation and promotion amidst the celebration.

"While the campus was beautiful, with its basic structures set between the hills and river shore, there were serious flaws in the map of the school grounds, not the least of which was a main public road that ran through the heart of the campus, where 'outsiders' from Route 341 and Route 7 could tear through the school on their way to Schaghticoke and race down the back road to Dog Tail Corners and Bull's Bridge.

"To allow access to the heart of campus for teachers and their families, the rich vegetable gardens that had occupied the river-washed land below the wall were removed and the current, narrow road was installed, complete with the 'thank you-ma'am speed bumps' to deter those who wanted a speedy shortcut to Schaghticoke.

"The Rectory—that long, low Frank Lloyd Wright kind of home that sits just a little north of the Bell Tower on Chapel Hill—was not there then either. A beautiful Cape Cod house, with a porch that looked down on "Club Norge" and the Housatonic was there. That house was picked up, sans the front porch and balcony, and moved down that steep hill with the sharp bend in it, to its present site on the Skiff Mountain Road in that little settlement of faculty houses north of the football fields. The Rectory, which had been located in the lower apartment of the north wing of the Middle Dorm, was built beside the bell tower. It was designed by Father Patterson himself, an architect before his ordination in 1934.

"Likewise, the Boathouse of the famous Kent Crew (*Life* Magazine, May 31, 1937, and *Life* Magazine, June 28, 1948) was originally situated on Schaghticoke Road across Macedonia Brook from the back of the Dining Hall. To build a new one in the current location adjacent to the varsity football field required that the homes that had been there, the William "Study Is Hard Work"

Armstrong family at the south end, the Ralph K. "English Studies" Ritchie family in the middle and the Bill "Head of Facility Maintenance" Parcells family in the north end, be moved north on Skiff Mountain Road, as part of the family settlement with the newly situated Chapel Hill Cape Cod house, still complete with its diamond shaped windows in the south sun room. Those diamond-shaped windows were from the original Kent chapel before St. Joseph's was built.

"The original gymnasium on the other side of the varsity football field was inadequate for everything that went on there, housing wrestling, intra-mural basketball and varsity basketball, plus football dressing rooms below—the atmosphere throughout wonderfully marinated with the smell of sweat, old and new—so a new extension to the Field House was built on the south end— the varsity basketball court, complete with the new aroma of varnished floors and paint, and sky lights to allow for sunlight to help light the building, not that it was very effective, given that the winter sun hid behind Mt. Algo by 4:00 PM throughout the length of the basketball season. At least passersby on Route 341 could tell when there was someone in the basketball court by the interior light coming through the skylights to the outside.

"Rather than continue to rely on the good graces of Kent's winter snows and cold air, a reliance that was sometimes ill-founded in the January thaws just as Kent Hockey was about to challenge Hotchkiss and Choate, the old system of hockey rinks was phased out. That system consisted of Chick Downs, Floyd Freeman, Ralph Ritchie, Smokey Smith, Manual "Misty" Nadal and others erecting three-foot high boards in the shape of hockey rinks on snow-covered baseball diamonds, football fields and soccer fields and then flooding them with water via fire hoses. Cherry noses and cheeks and numbed hands and toes were testament to and mementoes of their dedication, which had to be repeated after every event so that the ice would be smooth the next day. That travail and reliance on a fickle Mother Nature led to many defeats at the hands of said Hotchkiss, Choate and others which led to the raising of money for a long, man-made 'dike' at the base of Mt. Algo just a stone's throw south of Macedonia Brook and fed by the mountain streams of Mt. Algo."

We are also constantly aware of the important place which our athletic program must hold. It is a real satisfaction to find that for the first time in the School's history every boy not restricted by the physician is participating in sports each season. It is obvious that we must develop more adequate facilities for this expanded program and the four new hockey rinks

Above: The Chapel Hill cottage in which the Wests lived.

Below: The Rectory designed by Father Patterson.

Above left: Laying the cornerstone for the boathouse and the Sill oar.
Above right: The boathouse with the Sill oar.

mark step number one in the development. It is hoped that by next year the new club football and soccer fields will be ready for use. Expansion of the Sports Building, adequate boat houses, and other athletic needs are on our program for the future. From the earliest days Kent's reputation for the sportsmanship of its first teams has been outstanding. That spirit is being spread to every team in the club system and it is our determination that from now on it will be an experience available to every boy in School.

"The library used to be in the center section of the Middle Dorm—not a great deal of space even using the upper and lower levels. John Gray 'Bronx' Park, Kent '28 was the nattily dressed, quiet librarian/overseer for that library and the move of everything to the second floor of the Schoolhouse building. The move made the Middle Dorm the home for art shows, Sunday chess matches and debates on the upper floor and the place for tea dances and the Art History classes of one eccentric, but highly dedicated teacher, James H. Breasted. Mr. Breasted

Below left: The diamond-shaped window panes were originally in the wooden St. Joseph's Chapel. Today they grace a faculty home on Skiff Mountain Road.
Below right: The field house and the boathouse.

John Gray Park '28

John Gray Park entered Kent in November 1923, two months after the term had begun. "An incident his first day at school had a lasting effect." His answer – or lack thereof – to the question posed by Robert Wagner '24, the head of the table to which he was assigned, "What is your name, Park? Van Courtland or Bronx?" led to his being known as Bronx Park throughout his Kent career. As a student he played form hockey and he served as manager of the 1927 crew, the first American schoolboy eight to row at Henley. After a year at Harvard, he returned to Kent to begin his long career on the faculty. He took full charge of the Second Form. His obituary in the *Kent News* tells the story. He saw that the second form boys got to bed on time, got up and washed and dressed on time, and generally adjusted to the rigors of Kent life. He started a junior hockey team, and when a member of the English department became ill, Bronx stepped in. But what signaled his greatest contribution was his starting his own collection of books in his room, and making them available to all the students.

John Gray Park '28.

When the Middle Dorm was planned with new rooms he started a campaign for donations to the library, which brought in hundreds of volumes, crowned by the gift of 6,000 books by the late Burton F. White '19.

Bronx Park joined the Army Air Force in WWII, serving first as head of the intelligence school for enlisted men of the A.A.F. in Salt Lake City and late, with the rank of major, at the A.A.F. Personnel Distribution Command in Louisville, in connection with which he conducted a personnel survey of the Air Transport Command, which required 30,000 miles of travel in the Pacific area.

When he returned to Kent, he gave up teaching to concentrate on creating a fine library. When Mattison Auditorium was completed, the library moved to the former auditorium in the Schoolhouse. When the Girls School opened, he set up the separate division of the library on the Hill campus. But while all this took much of his time, he continued coaching in the club system.

Outside of School, he served as chairman of the library committee of the Secondary Education Board, forerunner of the National Association of Independent Schools, and as chairman of the legislative committee of the Connecticut Library Association. He also was a member, by appointment of the governor of Connecticut, in 1961-1963, on a special Commission on the Libraries of Connecticut.

John Gray Park was remembered by all who knew him as "a man of great personal modesty, yet one with firm convictions on what was right, and what was appropriate; a man who would fight stubbornly for what he felt was best for the students and for the school. They remember a man who had a deep personal interest in boys and their problems; a man who with quiet sympathy and understanding was a source of help and strength to those who sought his guidance. Upon his retirement on Prize Day 1971 the library at the Boys School was named the John Gray Park '28 Library and dedicated to his honor." (Excerpted from the obituary in the *Kent News*, April 22, 1972.)

The new library in Schoolhouse.

Above: Mattison Auditorium.

was the often-announced first American boy to enter King Tut's Tomb and he delivered his precise evening lectures on Art History complete with the mother-lode of his own perfectly photographed works of art from every part of the world. It was all something that few of us appreciated until years later.

"The current library, meanwhile, in the Schoolhouse, was used back then as an assembly hall and movie theatre on Saturday nights, complete with hard, folding wood chairs that were noisy on the bare wood floors—and hard. No one really missed that old auditorium and all appreciated the new (in 1955) Mattison Auditorium that was complete with softer, auditorium-style seats—lots of them.

"So, the lovely valley land of Kent became a little lovelier, a little more self-reliant and it was now secluded from public traffic which was now routed around the back leg of the Triangle.

"There were times of difficult decisions for Father Patterson and his administration. In addition to being a fundraiser par excellence and owner of a dairy farm, the Headmaster had to keep the academic standards competitive. Father Patterson and Kent had to make choices about getting teachers with national stature, which necessitated the replacement of some of Kent's teachers of long standing. With the decisions made, the actions were bold and direct, bringing in people of some national renown to serve and lead as department chairs."

And so it is that we are always striving to strengthen our faculty. A school is only as strong as the men who teach in it. An effective master at Kent is one who constantly thinks of his work as a ministry. It makes little difference whether his discipline be languages or mathematics, history or science—he must see the classroom as an area in which a facet of the one great truth is presented, not to a class but to a group of individuals, each unique, each important.

We are conscious of the needs of curriculum development. This does not mean that we anticipate adding numerous courses, for our concern is with the basic disciplines which traditionally constitute secondary education. It does mean that we must be conscious of new developments within each subject, and of new and improved methods of presentation. The goal of the Kent curriculum is not to get boys into college. It is not to develop certain skills. Kent is neither a cram school nor a vocational school. Our concern is not merely that our boys "know how" but rather that they "know why."

CAROLINE CIABURRI GILLIAM

After Caroline Gilliam died in October 1999, the *Kent Quarterly* reported "Kent seems an emptier place since [Caroline's death]. For so many years she had been a part of the School and the town, a part of all the lives she had met, no matter how briefly. Caroline came to Kent in the 1930s as the registered nurse in the infirmary and later married R. Lee Gilliam, history and music master at the School. When the Gilliams retired, they were sorely missed." In the years that followed, Caroline continued to be busy, volunteering at the Kent Nutrition Center and the New Milford Thrift Shop, helping with functions at St. Andrew's and participating in activities at the First Congregational Church and St. Bridget's as well.

Caroline Ciaburri Gilliam, 1948.

"First and foremost, Caroline Gilliam was for generations of Kent students a surrogate mother. Her ability to see through the imaginary ailments of students wishing to avoid a test or a job, coupled with her gift for comforting the truly afflicted and the homesick, provided Kent alumni with numerous stories of her ministry in the old infirmary. Don Gowan '66 remembers: 'She was the kind of lady you never forget. She was a blunt lady who spoke her mind; at the same time she had a terrific sense of humor and a sense of what was needed. She wasn't ashamed to tell you if you needed a haircut, if you had gained weight or if you simply looked tired.' O.B. Davis '42 remembers her as being a strict bouncer for the infirmary. 'Malingerers were quickly sent away, and in her eyes we were all potential malingerers.' However, Caroline's strictness was simply one side of the real concern she felt for her boys, and her nurturing side revealed itself in the pies and cakes she baked for them. Her Texas brownies; (rich chocolate cake covered in layers of chocolate icing) were especially famous.

" . . . Stuyvie Bearns '55 [remembers] her extraordinary warmth, her ability as head nurse and her amazing talents as a diagnostician. 'I arrived late at Kent in September of 1950 . . . About a week after arriving, I was struck suddenly by a grievous illness and literally ran to the infirmary. In the hallway, I encountered Mrs. Gilliam. She encountered a 97-pound, four-foot-eleven, 13-year-old convulsed in tears. Her rapid assessment noted no deformities, bruises, blood or apparent trauma. Her diagnosis was immediate and 100 percent accurate: potentially terminal homesickness. She quickly administered the only known cure, sweeping me up from the floor in a hug I recall vividly today and pouring down a solid dose of motherly love as she held me in her arms. She followed this with 20 minutes of cocoa therapy on the porch of the infirmary, and when I had calmed down she sent me back through the door to the serious business of getting myself educated.'

"It truly can be said that Caroline Gilliam had a way of evoking the best in those whose lives she helped to shape. Stuyvie Bearns became her lawyer some seven or eight years before she died, and he enjoyed his visits with her when they shared a cup of tea or glass of wine. She would ask him what made the world so wonderful and then say that it was people like him. He said, 'She did this little ritual with everyone . . . but we all knew she was wrong, 180 degrees wrong, because it wasn't and isn't people like me. It was and is people like her who made you realize what John was getting at in the Gospel and Epistles when he said "God is love." Because it is through people like Caroline that we receive that love and all of her thousands of sons and daughters from Kent School who knew her and felt that love never, ever will forget it.'"

Caroline Gilliam truly was a loving, generous, firm presence in the lives of those who knew her.

RICHARD LEE GILLIAM

Richard Lee Gilliam, Gillie, taught European history and directed the Glee Clubs, Choir, Kentones, and Kentettes. His many talents are remembered today by those whose lives he touched and continues to touch.

"When the chapel breaks into the lyrics of poet Robert Hillyer and begins singing 'The haze on Algo's height is rent . . .' they sing the music of R. Lee Gilliam, vocal master at Kent School from 1928-1973.

"By definition a master at Kent School is involved in numerous activities, and Mr. Gilliam was no exception. A temporary position as history teacher developed into a full-time appointment, and led Gilliam back to numerous graduate courses at Harvard, Columbia, NYU, and inspired a trip to Europe at the outbreak of World War II. He became a teacher of European history for whom his chairman of 39 years, William Worthington, thinks only the word 'great' is sufficient. During the war years Mr. Gilliam led military drills and helped Bill Nadal coach varsity basketball and baseball. It was Lee Gilliam's mellifluous voice which Yale University chose to narrate their recorded history of the 1956 American presidential campaign. For years Mr. Gilliam selected the concerts and films which were presented at Kent School."

Following Gillie's death, his widow, Caroline, received numerous letters from his former students, *"expressing the lasting positive influence"* he had on them.

Jim Mell '60 wrote "'My memories are so fond of him as a teacher of history whose wit and attention to detail made the subject an exciting experience (I majored in European history later on); as a musician who tolerantly, dedicatedly, and again with great humor inspired an appreciation of choral music never surpassed by future teachers I had . . . and most of all as friend and advisor.'" Neil Keller Biddle '64 wrote "'His music and the music he helped us make, as well as his love and caring support, brought much joy into the lives of so many of us little people far from home.'"

Lee Gilliam was a strong advocate of the music program that he did so much to create at Kent. In a letter to Father Patterson he wrote, "'The day is long past when music can be treated as a mere appendage—something one does when there is nothing else to do, or, if there is any time left, let's give it to the chorus, or, let them give a concert if they can wedge it in an already crowded schedule of athletic events, or if there is any space left, regardless of its location, let's move the piano there . . . It is imperative that we do

Caroline and Lee Gilliam.

all we can to keep the subject alive and interesting for all concerned.'

"In the decades which followed, Kent singing groups experienced a renaissance which gained national attention thanks to the strong leadership of R. Lee Gilliam. It was typical of the complete dedication of his teaching career that even after he retired he continued to work with the school's vocal groups. His statement in a 1975 letter to Headmaster Towle could well stand as a statement of the strength of character and commitment which built Kent School.

"'In my mind, teaching has never been merely a life work, a profession, a job, but rather a passion. The greatest part of my compensation has been the joy of spending my professional life in, or near a community of students, alumni and fellow-faculty members.'" (excerpted from the *Kent News*, "Richard Lee Gilliam: 1902-1984," by Judson Scruton).

"Robert E.K. Rourke and Henry Syer came to lead a strong Math Department while James H. Breasted, son of the world renowned archeologist formed a special department and discipline on art history in a college lecture format. They added to the core faculty that included William Worthington, who was active in town and state politics; Edmund Fuller, *The Wall Street Journal's* chief book critic, noted writer for *The New York Times, The New York Herald-Tribune,* and the *Saturday Review of Literature* and teacher; Lee Gilliam, composer of the Kent School Song; Caroline Ciaburri Gilliam, his wife who was the nurse of the infirmary, whose commanding voice could be heard regularly and diligently encouraging boys to walk tall, 'Head up, shoulders back… that's a-boy.'

"William H. Armstrong, creator of the special discipline of Study, became a legend in his own time for his hard discipline, writing talents and slogans re: work (A man who does only what is expected of him is a slave; the moment he does more than what is expected, he is a free man.) Rising at 3:00 AM, he read *Chaucer, The Holy Bible,* and other works and did his own writing which included *Study Is Hard Work* and *Sounder,* which was made into a movie that was nominated for an Academy Award.

Left: William Armstrong: "Study is hard work!"

Dr. Henry W. Syer

Dr. Syer came to Kent to teach mathematics in 1958, and in 1962 he became chairman of the Mathematics Department. On the occasion of his retirement in 1980, Ted Morse, chairman of the History Department, paid tribute to him.

Henry Syer.

"Whereas, Henry W. Syer, graduate of Harvard College Summa cum Laude, and Doctor of Education from the same institution, has amassed a Malthusian list of credits, publications, and imaginatively creative ways of making the science of mathematics palpable, interesting, and intellectually challenging. Through his years as instructor at the Gunnery School, Culver Military Academy, Boston University, and Kent School, Henry has emerged as a pillar of regional and national leadership through textbook writing, use of the media, and in the academic training of aspiring teachers. His co-authorship with Robert Rourke of *Algebra I* in 1967 has become a staple in private and public education. His imaginative seizure of the idea that filmstrips and visual mathematical tools could aid young students was pioneered as early as 1945. . . . For those of us at Kent, we know the internal warmth, good cheer, spirit of service and dedication that Henry has shown as department chairman, member of the faculty committee, and chairman of every difficult assignment that the rest of us would prefer to sidestep. . . .. I move that we offer a resolution saluting a life of compelling curiosity, a life which does not coincide with one of his geometric theorems. For Henry Syer, there is no proven, no Q.E.D. There are more things to be investigated" (*Kent News,* October 4, 1980).

"Dr. Syer's passion for education fueled a tireless passion to instill in even the most reluctant scholar a firm understanding of the basic principles of algebra and geometry, logic and analysis. At the same time, his encyclopedic mind provided limitless sustenance to those eager to advance their knowledge and skill. . . The door of the Syer home was always open. His advisees and the many other students, parents, and teachers who sought his advice or company there will remember the cordial welcome always ready, and the inexhaustible supply of anecdotes, homilies, and humor" (Thomas K. Roney, *Kent News,* April 1989).

"Even so, the future was being planned, shaped and put into action. A shiny face on a renewed campus and happy faculty and staff were not the hallmarks of the greatness that was still being implemented. It was slow in coming, but the world of Kent was beginning to reach out to the world at large. It was in the mid-fifties that the first non-white student was admitted at Kent School. Lowell Johnston was varsity football, varsity basketball, and first crew. What is more, he was tapped and took on the responsibilities as a prefect, to the high approval of his classmates and teachers. He went on to Harvard Law.

"Later, a Korean student named Teddy Sinn came to Kent, and a Japanese student, Sukeyoshi (nicknamed Yo-chun) Yamamoto came, too. Yo-chun later wrote a book, *Dearest Mother,* based on his letters to his mother while he was a student at Kent. The book became a best seller in Japan (ranked 3rd for non-fiction in 1961) and made Kent famous in Japan.

"These moves were quietly implemented, but in the world of the '50's, these moves were bold and daring. Under a strong administration captained by a strong Father Patterson, they came about smoothly and fruitfully.

"As if all of that were not enough, Kent celebrated its fiftieth year of operation, education and growth in 1956. Father Patterson orchestrated a full year of extraordinary review, evaluation and strategic planning. Throughout that year, Kent hosted a series of panels on the concept of 'The Christian Idea of Education,' serving up some of the most noted minds from a worldwide Christian and education community, including Alan Paton, one of the strong and forward-looking, brave and adventuresome souls of world class social change who engineered the end to apartheid in South Africa. It ended with a grand week in June 1956 when people from the Kent Family, past, present and some future, plus educators worldwide, the Kent Village Community and interested others gathered at Kent and in the town of Kent and at South Kent School (founded by Father Sill and two Kent alumni) for

Above: Alan Paton. Lensk photograph from the jacket of Tales from a Troubled Land, *Charles Scribner's Sons, 1961.*

parties, receptions, lectures, and a Eucharist celebrated in a specially created Sanctuary erected on the varsity soccer field, complete with the huge crucifix brought from the front wall of St. Joseph's to hang over the alfresco sanctuary altar. The grandeur of the altar and Sanctuary were not an overestimate for the crowds that came to that Sunday celebration. Nor were there too few celebrants on hand, even though Kent had never seen so many ordained people at any one time before, their vestments flowing impressively as they walked about the open air Sanctuary."

The face of Kent had changed in the seven quick years from John Oliver Patterson's arrival at Kent to the memorable Fiftieth Anniversary Celebration. The '50s were also years of academic growth, for in March 1956, Father Patterson inaugurated The Guild, "an organization designed to give a student who has exceptional ability a chance to share his interests, curiosity, and knowledge with others. . . . Membership in The Guild will be the highest honor a student can

Below: The Eucharist celebrating the 50th anniversary of the founding of the School, 1956.

attain" (*Kent News*, March 1, 1956). The five department heads were permanent members of the organization, and each student member was to be nominated by one of these heads and then accepted by the others. Criteria were excellence in a particular subject as well as satisfactory work in all other subjects the nominee was studying. Only fifth and sixth formers were eligible. The first meeting of The Guild was held on March 5. Nine students were

As part of the celebration of Kent's fiftieth year, Alan Paton wrote a prayer.

Prayer
For the Use of One in Authority
(Written for a Kent Headmaster)

My plan be in Thy Mind, O God
My work be in Thy hands
My ears be ever swift to hear
The words of Thy commands.

My feet be ever swift to run
When I am called by Thee
My hands be ever swift to do
The task thou givest me.

Oh may my weak and earth-blind eyes
Be ever swift to see
Thine image in each son of Thine
Thou dost commit to me.

Dwell Thou in every hall and room
In every head and heart
Walk thou the roads and fields of Kent
That Kent be where Thou art.

Be pleased the bounty of thy grace
On this Thy School to pour
As Thou hast done these fifty years
Do Thou these fifty more.

named as charter student members: sixth formers Bert Waters, Frank Beane, Winslow Harris, Blair Bigelow, John Hawkins, and Russell Wing and fifth formers Nicholas Joukovsky, Merrill Bailey, and Peter Schwindt. Alan Paton introduced the evening's speaker, Father Trevor Huddleston, who spoke on "Personal Responsibility." It was an auspicious beginning.

And so Kent will justify its existence and claim to be a church school in direct ratio to the extent to which in classroom and laboratory, in chapel and dormitory, on the playing fields or the auditorium stage, in the study hall or at the master's desk, every lesson studied or prayer offered, every game played or rule announced, every assignment fulfilled or lecture prepared, is done for the glory of God and the wholeness of his people.

Let us not make the mistake of looking at such a program as being too soberly pious or discouragingly difficult for achievement. It has not been so in the past and it will not be so in the future. The goal of Christian Education is to give men motive and strength for mature living. Certainly such education demands joy, certainly the pursuit of such living requires play. Chesterton points out that "joy which was the small publicity of the pagan is the gigantic secret of the Christian." That such joy-such true fun-has always been a characteristic of life at Kent will be verified by every alumnus who was ever truly been a part of the community.

"Simplicity of Life was and is a continuing tenant of Kent School, but even so, it was getting more complicated as Kent reached out to diversify. It was said, some years back by people who are gone now, that Fr. Sill had faced some lean years, even perilously disastrous years financially. Pater never saw it, and probably never designed any of the plans to fulfill his pledge, but quietly, behind the scenes, plans were laid, more money was solicited and given and the Rawson Farm property atop Skiff Mountain was acquired so that in the fall of 1960, a Girls Division of The Kent School for Boys was opened. It was done with strength, executed privately, calmly and effectively over many years through skillful planning and administration. Once again, Kent was a leader, now establishing coordinated education for boys and girls in private boarding schools.

"In 1961, Fr. Patterson took a Sabbatical year. He went off for a year of rest, reflection and envisioning of the future from his own eyes . . . He returned to Kent—after one 'whale of a vacation'—in June 1962 to announce that he was leaving Kent to found St. Stephen's School in Rome, Italy, in collaboration with Raydon P. Ronshaugen and Robert E. K. Rourke, members of the Kent staff. St. Stephen's School, he said, would be driven on the same lines as Kent, complete with crew. The school continues today, having been led by Arthur "Ron" Tooman (Kent '53) as the second headmaster.

Above: Father Patterson overseeing building on the Skiff Mountain campus for the girls school.

"By then, Kent School was working according to plan, with students still running the government of the school and students taking responsibility for the continuation of life simply, directly and reliantly." (Michael H. West '62 grew up at Kent, the son of the Reverend Samuel West, Chaplain and Assistant Headmaster from 1949 to 1959.)

When we can bring to our sons and daughters a respect for that which is excellent, for that which is fine, for that which (in a true and lasting sense) is of eternal validity in every field, then we will have solved one of the greatest problems in the world of today. It is, I submit, an enterprise that must start in the home if it is ever to succeed in the school.

The enterprise starts as we are willing to look at and listen to what the centuries before us have seen to be fine and important and meaningful. It starts as we frankly and openly know that real men are never ashamed or scornful of beauty, of decency, of intelligence or truth. It moves on in an effort to show our children their own capacities as creative, responsible persons in whatsoever fields God has endowed them. The enterprise will determine to touch each child's conscience in such a way that he will never be content with what he knows to be the tawdry and the second-rate. It will constantly strive to give each child an acquaintance with the heroes of all ages, in all fields so that his picture of man is not provincial and suburban. Its goal is to give him a base of important and essential knowledge, to cap this with a sense of the harmony and the inter-relation of all truth, and to crown this with a philosophy and theology that gives him an understanding of meaning and value. Its goal is not to make him a skilled or secure man—its goal is to make him an educated man. Its goal is not Main Street, but rather eternal life.

Father Patterson served as headmaster of St. Stephen's until his retirement in 1970. He continued his work in the church in Rome, serving as an associate priest of the Episcopal Church of St. Paul-within-the-walls. In 1978, he and his wife moved to San Francisco, where he became a part time associate at St. James parish. In February 1988 during a national liturgical conference concerning the work to restore the ancient Catechumenate for "Christian Formation," Father Patterson, Dr. Massey H. Shepherd, Jr., and Dr. Samuel E. West were honored

THE SCHOOL SONGS

Kent has had two school songs. The first one, "There's a River Through a Valley," written in 1907 by William H. Whittington, one of the first masters, and sung at least until 1947, and "The Haze on Algo's Height," written by Robert Hillyer '13, which in 1947 apparently became more popular. An editorial in *The Kent News* on October 29, 1947, put the case for both of them.

Ever since a member of the Kent faculty set "The Haze on Algo's Height" to music some years ago, the song has been well-liked and popular among members of the student body and alumni association. . . . The song was written by one of our most illustrious alumni and a member of the faculty set it to music, thus creating a living song with connections to our tradition. . . . Perhaps some sort of arrangement could be worked out whereby both songs would have definite places in the Kent tradition, for they both have points in their favor. "There's a River" is close to the hearts of the older classes, and "The Haze" means more to recent alumni.

Here are both of the songs of Pater's school.

THERE'S A RIVER THROUGH A VALLEY

There's a river through a valley,
And nearby that river-side
There's a place we'll all remember
When we've scattered far and wide;
We'll recall it with affection,
We'll recall it too with pride.
Of our own Kent School we now are singing,
To our own Kent School we now are bringing
This tribute to her rule, send it ringing,
'Till the echoes fling it hither to abide.

Here we stand for what is worthy,
Here we stand for what is right,
And our hopes being in the future,
Let us make that future bright;
While our School is here to help us
With a clear and steady light;
Of our own Kent School we now are singing
To our own Kent School we now are bringing,
This tribute to her rule, send it ringing,
'Till the echoes fling it hither day and night.

THE HAZE ON ALGO'S HEIGHT

The haze on Algo's height is rent,
Morning unsheathes her fiery sword,
The lovely valley land of Kent,
Comes forth in light to hail her Lord;
How fair upon the waking slope,
The promise of the morning lies,
And fair in waking hearts, the hope
That climbs the bright auroral skies.

Always the valley flows with day,
Always the hills of morning stand,
Always the faith more strong than they,
Will bear their voice from land to land.
O heart that wakes in young content,
Between the hills and river shore,
Remember still thy dawn at Kent,
'Till dawn and darkness are no more.

as three of the four co-founders and charter-signers of Associated Parishes. John Oliver Patterson died on November 12, 1988, in San Francisco, California. O.B. Davis said, for the *Kent News* (January 28, 1989): "He was a man of remarkably vigorous intellect who urged Kent toward academic excellence. He sought and found first rate faculty, instituted such enhanced academic demands as a tutorial reading program for all students, and required active participation by everybody in school sponsored lecture and seminar series. The success of his insistence that Kent emphasize sound learning and intellectual attainment has, without question, remained one of John Patterson's important contributions to this school." In the same issue of the *News*, Father Schell wrote: "A dwindling handful remains who worked here while John Patterson was active as Rector and Headmaster of Kent School. These few have particular reasons to be thankful for Father Patterson's life and work, the special advantages of having been witness to his remarkable eloquence, vision, and devotion. These few who have known him as great priest and friend are fortunate among us. But most of us here now started our Kent life after 1962. In person we have known John Oliver Patterson in the flesh only if we have been lucky enough to encounter him during his few visits to the school. Everyone here at Kent, however, owes grateful honor to John Patterson as a historic headmaster who maintained and enlarged Kent's identity as a school of Christian purpose, who by imaginative and strenuous endeavor turned Kent sharply in the direction of the more serious scholarly emphasis that he saw coming times to require. He was and remains a Kent hero, his literal portrait enshrined in the dining hall, his good works on our behalf enshrined in the heart of the School. Thank God for the life of John Oliver Patterson and may light perpetual shine upon him."

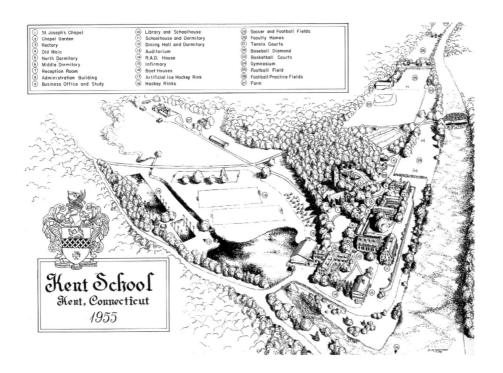

THE FARM

ONE OF THE ASPECTS OF KENT THAT MADE THE SCHOOL unique was the farm. Early issues of the *Kent School News* reported regularly on the potato crop, the fall haying, and the number of bushels of apples picked. Farm work continued in the summer—of necessity—and then into the fall haying season. "There was an excellent hay crop, more than the barn could hold. The oats were harvested at just the right time. They had fine full heads. The corn also proved a record crop. . . The potato crop is still to be harvested. In connection with the summer's work it is interesting to note that already over 2000 quart jars of fruit and vegetables have been preserved, most of the coming from the school yield" (9/27/18).

Later that fall, on November 1, the *News* reported that forty barrels of apples were picked by Kent boys and "brought down Skiff Mountain in three separate all-day trips. One of the most important items of outside work done by the fellows has been that of apple-picking. We are very fortunate in getting any apples at all, but the school was able to buy forty barrels from Mr.

McGlashan on Skiff Mountain. These were picked by the fellows and in this way the school obtained them for two dollars a barrel. The trees were fine low ones, almost breaking with their load of Baldwins, so the picking was comparatively easy. The start for home was made about at five o'clock, after Mrs. McGlashan had brought out either some warm gingerbread or some hot chocolate in preparation for the worst part of the expedition. The trip down the mountain was rather difficult, especially in the dark" (11/1/18).

The first Farm Manager was George Baker, who started to work at the School as a handyman. He came to Kent in the fall of 1908. He had been working at West Park, the home of the Holy Cross Monastery, in the vineyards when Father Sill asked "to borrow" him for the winter. His duties began as he drove some docile cows to Kent from somewhere near the Hudson in order to increase the size of the herd, which then numbered three. His days began when he turned on the blowers in the furnace room and lit the kitchen stove. He was named Farm Superintendent in 1910 and he kept that title until 1914 when Monk Wilson '08 returned to school to take over that position. George Baker continued to work at the school as manager of the Stock Room and general handyman. Perhaps the most important thing Baker did during his tenure was to contain the fire that had broken out in Mr. Worthington's classroom until help could arrive, thereby perhaps saving the building. He finally was forced to retire in April 1932 after he suffered a stroke.

Barry with a calf.

The farm.

however, the less we appreciate the value of this healthy drink. Today it is just a matter of course that we drink milk in much the same manner that water is consumed elsewhere, each person imbibing from two to three glasses per meal, besides the glass at recess feed. Likewise, many of the vegetables which we eat come from the farm, bringing nourishment to us who go to make up the School. . . . From these facts it is plain how great is the value of the farm, and how much it deserves the highest praise which we can give it, as a dominant agent in making us healthy, wealthy, and wise."

World War II caused a crisis of sorts on the farm as the farm hands were lured away by the high wages paid to factory workers. While all the area farms experienced this problem, only Kent School had 300 potential farm workers easily available. So Mr. Miller, the farm superintendent, spoke to the boys at an assembly, and "at least a hundred fellows volunteered for milking, despite the fact that this job required arising at four-thirty in the morning." Needless to say, it also required a certain skill, and gradually the milking squad was formed, two groups of three, two shifts weekly in the morning and two groups, two shifts in the afternoon. Dave Tirrel was the faculty supervisor of the farm hands, taking hours boys and anyone else who volunteered into the fields to do whatever needed to be done. The crisis was averted (*The Kent News,* April 29, 1942).

After the fire that destroyed the farm, the silo was the last building to go.

In October 1930, Mr. Miller, the head farmer at that time, reported that, despite a shortage of rain in the spring, the "vegetable gardens of beets, carrots, onions, potatoes, cabbage, and especially corn have thrived especially well. . . . The Kent herd, with a few exceptions, belongs to the Holstein family and . . . of the eighty now comprising our herd, only two were born outside our barns."

The lead editorial on January 28, 1931, credited the farm with having "a great deal to do with keeping the school in first-class condition. . . . Kent is famous for that health-builder, milk. When we first arrived here we were surprised at the abundance with which this fluid is served here at School. The longer we remain here,

Over the years, with the technological advances in farming and mechanization of many of the farm jobs, the involvement of the boys in the farm diminished, and by 1968, when all of the cows were milked by machine, the farm was operated by two men, the boys helping occasionally during harvest time and on weekends.

The School was especially proud of its herd of Holsteins. In April 1963, *The Kent News* reported that

Landmark Destroyed; Kent School Farm Burns Down

by David Sheppard '79

Sunday night, January 23, the Kent School Barn, the only remaining structure of the original wooden school, burned to the ground. The first alarm came at about 12:30 a.m. from a passing driver, though the barn had probably been burning for a while before that. Kent Fire Chief Robert Bauer and his company arrived moments later, but at that time the barn was over "fifty per cent involved." A total of four companies fought the fire in near-zero weather until 7:00 in the morning.

The barn housed the Kent School herd, which supplied milk for about 700 Kent School students, faculty, and families. Thirty-one cows and five calves died, most in the actual fire, but several animals had to be shot because they were in severe pain. The surviving cattle were taken to a farm in Wassaic, New York, several miles away, where they are being fed with feed from the School's silos, which were not harmed as they are cement block. The school is leasing the farm

in Dover, and the cows are milked daily. The milk is sent back to the school's pasteurizing plant to be processed for School use.

The area where the blaze started is known, but the cause remains un-

photo by Howard Weisman
Ice encases the charred remains of the Kent School Farm.

determined. A popular opinion was that of electrical fire, but the fire marshal found that there were no wires running anywhere near the

blaze's point of origin.

The barn was built by the school in 1911, on the site of the present day infirmary. The structure was moved to its present site in 1923, when the infirmary was built. Additions were made through the years, but the barn itself remained basically unchanged. According to Father Sill's statement in the Autumn 1911 **Kent Quarterly**, the barn was, at the time of its construction, the best in the county.

Whether the barn will be replaced is an undecided question. A joint meeting of the Trustees and the Alumni Council referred the question to the Executive Committee, whose decision pends on various questions, such as the cost of reconstruction. There is no official price tag yet, but Business Manager Richard Lindsay estimates the loss in terms of "a quarter of a million dollars." The decision of the Executive Committee should be forthcoming, but until such time as the decision is made, the cows will probably be moved to another farm in the immediate Kent area.

The Kent Farm in more tranquil times.

 Guild Paper Presented . . .

"Shinto - The Way Of The Gods"

by Felicity Costin

"Shinto, the national religion of Japan, is an ancient religion. It is similar to the Bronze Age forerunners of the classical Greek and Roman religions, although no relation between them has yet been proved," began Libby Webber's Guild Paper on the Shinto religion of Japan. Addressing a small group of faculty, students and relatives in the Alumni

combination of cults from various parts of Asia." The most influential cults which are apparent in Shinto are "shamanistic cults and hero- or ancestor-worship cults from the North, and fertility cults along with sun- and nature-worship cults from the South."

Another interesting fact in Libby's paper is that the Japanese, unlike the Greeks, did not fear their gods. Fear was basic to most early religions, but

Kent ⚜ News

VOL. 63, NO. 6 PUBLICATION, KENT SCHOOL, KENT, CT. RET. POSTAGE GUARANTEED SAT., FEB. 5, 1977

---

the herd had won two awards, the first for the whole herd for producing more milk per capita than any other herd in Litchfield County, the second for Kent School Roburke Paula, who had produced 19,000 pounds of milk and 664 pounds of butterfat in 264 days. Roburke Paula received the Curtiss Gold Seal Award for this remarkable feat. Lest this seem a trivial point to make in a centennial history of the School, one has to remember that the herd, and Paula, described in the *News* as "a 1300 pound beauty," supplied the boys and girls, masters and their families, with "nature's perfect food." The farm was a serious business and an integral part of Kent for many of its 100 years.

All of this came to an end on the night of January 23, 1977, when the School barn, "the only remaining structure of the original wooden school, burned to the ground. . . . The barn housed the Kent School herd, which supplied milk for about 700 Kent School students, faculty, and families. Thirty-one cows and five calves died, . . . and the surviving cattle were taken to a farm in Wassaic, New York. . . ." In May 1977, the Trustees decided not to rebuild the barn, and the cows were sold in July and the old foundations of the barn and the silo were demolished. The days when Kent had its own farm had come to an end.

IV
The New Proceeding
from the Old

By THE END OF 1957 THE STAGE WAS SET FOR THE NEXT MAJOR CHANGE in the life of Kent School. The board decided to authorize extensive studies of ways in which Kent might take affirmative steps to advance the cause of Christian independent school education. At its meeting on September 20, 1957, Board President Beaumont Whitney '15 announced that he had appointed Cy Vance '35, who had recently been elected to the board, to be chairman of a special alumni committee, which had a threefold mission: to study the ways in which Kent School might better use its facilities in the cause of Christian and independent school education; to study the desirability and feasibility of establishing another boys school of Christian intent; and the desirability and feasibility of establishing a girls school of Christian intent. The members of the Vance Committee were Hadley Case '29, C. Stedman Chandler '21, G. Barron Mallory '37, Osgood Perry '08, Dominic W. Rich '14, Whitney North Seymour, Jr. '41, Olcott D. Smith '25, John B. Stevens '33, Louis T. Stone '33, Sidney N. Towle '31, W. Beaumont Whitney II '15, and Cyrus R. Vance '35.

At the November meeting of the Vance Committee, Sidney Towle presented a report on the progress of subcommittee C, to which was delegated the problem of determining the desirability of establishing a girls school affiliate of Kent. In March 1958, Mr. Towle reported that the full committee had agreed that, were a girls school to be created, it should provide a "parallel education, not coeducation; (and that) …there should be a single headmaster, but two separate principals to supervise administrative problems, (and) …single department heads to provide a unified curriculum…. (Furthermore) insofar as possible, the faculty at the girls school should consist of approximately equal distribution of male and female teachers."

At this time, he also reported that the Rawson farm on Skiff Mountain had come on the market and would be a suitable site for a girls school. This meeting proved to be pivotal, for the Board unanimously passed the following resolution:

> RESOLVED that the Board of Trustees endorses in principle
> the idea of establishing a girls school of Christian intent and
> authorizes the Vance Committee: a) To draw up rough plans for

Above: Father Patterson and Mr. Towle on the river.

the establishment of a girls school in the vicinity of Kent, including the requirements of staff, plant and curriculum, and; b) To assemble an informal committee to consider means of raising the necessary funds to establish such proposed school....

At Pater's Birthday Dinner on March 14, Father Patterson reported on college admissions, the huge number of applications for admission to Kent, and the many factors considered before a boy was accepted. But even more important for the future of Kent School was the subject of discussion the next day, March 15, when the board of trustees and the alumni council held a joint meeting at the Harvard Club. Cy Vance reported on the work done by his committee to study the responsibilities of Kent School in the cause of Christian and independent school education. His remarks were contained in a series of resolutions adopted by the board at their March 14 meeting. The principal points were reported in the *Kent News* of April 17, 1958, and the one that changed Kent forever was "that the Board of Trustees endorses in principle the idea of establishing a girls school of Christian intent and authorizes the Vance Committee (a) to draw up rough plans for the establishment of a girls school in the vicinity of Kent . . . (b) to assemble an informal committee to consider means of raising the necessary funds. . . ."

By September, the Vance Committee had proposed that Kent's program be expanded to include the education of girls and the Board had unanimously approved the proposal. It was quite clear, however, that the proposal was for a girls department with a separate faculty, separate facilities, and separate classes. As the *Kent News* reported, Father Patterson's report made it clear that "[t]his system would offer the many great advantages and none of the possible disadvantages of co-education." The *News* went on to report that the girls division would be based on certain policies which were still being discussed:

"(1) The Rector and Headmaster of Kent will be Rector of both schools and a Principal will be appointed for the girls division. (2) Kent will offer a four-year college preparatory course following in general the existing curriculum at Kent. (3) The department chairmen of Kent will serve as department chairmen for the

Below: The Rawson farm. Some of the buildings in the picture became schoolrooms.

separate girls faculty. It is planned that approximately 50% of the new faculty will be men. (4) The two divisions will use basically the same admissions and tuition policies. The majority of students admitted will undertake a four-year course. (5) A substantial program for 'self-help' will be instituted with strong emphasis on student responsibility. (6) The girls department will open with two forms (third and fourth forms) with about 50 students in each. At the end of each of the first two years an additional form will be established looking toward a student body of 200."

CYRUS R. VANCE '35
A MAN FOR ALL SEASONS

Cyrus R. Vance '35 lived the School's motto—Simplicity of Life, Directness of Purpose, and Self-reliance—on behalf of America. Cy was a son of West Virginia, Kent and Yale, and during his years at the School, he was senior prefect, a member of the football team, a hockey player, and a member of the 1934 crew that went to Henley. In one of the many obituaries that appeared following his death, *The Times* (London) wrote: "If he did not conform to all the stereotypes of the East Coast Establishment, it could perhaps be attributed to his birthplace, West Virginia. His father, who was of Welsh ancestry and who died when his son was just five, was an insurance executive. Nevertheless, Vance's education had the stamp of privilege: Kent (one of the country's most exclusive schools), then Yale, where he suffered a back injury while captaining the university hockey team."

Cy truly belonged to the world. As his obituary in *The New York Times* noted, he served his country in myriad ways, most prominently perhaps as Secretary of State from 1977 to 1980. Kent is immensely proud of her son, who made a difference in the 20th century, and we join the world in celebrating this man, an internationally known statesman. We also celebrate the man who helped to change the very nature of Kent School: Cyrus Vance, chairman of the Vance Committee, which brought about the founding of the Girls School. Without the vision and work of Vance and his committee, Kent might be a very different place today.

On January 19, 2002, the world bade farewell to Cyrus R. Vance at the Episcopal Church of the Heavenly Rest in New York City. Among those who paid tribute to him were Theodore Sorensen and Dr. Henry Kissinger. In his eulogy, Dr. Kissinger said, "Cyrus Vance devoted his life to the service of his nation and the search for peace in the world. Dedicated, tenacious, unflappable, self-effacing, Cy was a gentleman of

Cyrus R. Vance '35.

what is now called 'the old school': We would all be better off had qualities such as his remained commonplace…. (The 1960s were) a time for Cy's special qualities: a dedication to the cause of freedom, total reliability, profound respect for different points of view. Above all, Cy stood for that special brand of American optimism that sees the Golden Age in the future, not in the past, and therefore never doubts that even the most daunting problems are solvable.

"Almost inevitably, Cy became the nation's indispensable troubleshooter. When thoughtful assessments and calm judgment were needed, he was called in: on Cyprus in 1967, on the Detroit conflagration in 1968 after the assassination of Martin Luther King, Jr., and on negotiations with the North Vietnamese in Paris. Given his service in the Pentagon, peace in Vietnam was a goal especially close to his heart. Caught in the dilemma between our commitments and our possibilities, he devoted himself to the task with understated passion…. His associates then and later spoke with affection and admiration about how he worked so meticulously, how he prepared himself so carefully, and how he would edit any memorandum to remove superlatives or the word 'very' and to modify any sentence that began with an 'I.' Cy served his nation and his principles, never himself; that is why he rarely talked about his service in the Navy during World War II. To Cy, doing one's duty was its own reward….

"The late great Ambassador Chip Bohlen used to quote from *Alice in Wonderland:* 'If you don't know where you are going, any road will get you there.' Cyrus Vance always knew where he was going. He will be laid to rest, by his choice, in Arlington National Cemetery among the comrades who, like him, each in his or her own way devoted their lives to service. It will be the end of a long journey that advanced the cause of peace, and brought honor to his country and decency to the world."

Theodore Sorensen compared Cy Vance to another

(continued)

great statesman, Sir Thomas More. "Nearly 500 years ago, Sir Thomas More—later to become Saint Thomas More—was the conscience of England's leadership and legal profession. A quiet, high-born gentleman, scholar and statesman, he placed principle above personal interest by refusing to support the king on an action Sir Thomas believed to be wrong. He resigned his high office instead. A devoted husband, grandfather and father, a generous friend, a man noted for his integrity and wisdom, he was termed by Samuel Johnson: 'The person of the greatest virtue these islands ever produced.' A contemporary called him a man with 'an angel's wit and singular learning, a man of gentleness and affability…of marvelous mirth as the time required and sometimes of sad gravity—a man for all seasons.' This sounds familiar to those of us who knew and loved Cy Vance….

"How best should we remember this extraordinary man? How would he have preferred to be remembered? Not by having his name engraved in marble on some giant edifice,

or inscribed upon a signboard above a massive highway or airport, but instead by engraving in the minds and memories of American foreign policymakers forevermore the basic principles of international relations best exemplified by the life and service of Cyrus Vance: a belief that cooperation with allies and neighbors is better than isolation or attempted domination; that communication between hostile parties is better than vituperation; and that negotiation is better than escalation.

"That is why I am certain that Cy today…is busy negotiating a treaty of friendship and commerce between heaven and hell, of course dealing directly with the CEO as he always did, and no doubt out-negotiating Lucifer, who is at a distinct disadvantage because he has no lawyers.

"But, in truth, no ordinary lawyer's words or wiles could overcome the virtues, the patience and the sheer goodness of Cyrus Vance, our country's own man for all seasons."

Below: (Top) The Rawson farm. This building became the headmasters residence. (Bottom) Drawing showing how the farm would be converted.

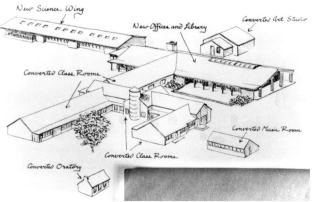

To make all of this possible, the Board had already purchased the Rawson Farm on Skiff Mountain. In October 1958 a proposed opening date of 1960 was announced. Father Sill's dream, which had been realized in the valley, was now about to be realized on the mountain.

The purchase of the 625-acre Rawson Farm seemed serendipitous in many ways. Hobart Rawson had died a year earlier, leaving the farm to his daughter, Mrs. Priscilla Young, the widow of Melvin Young '32, who had been killed in World War II (and for whom the Melvin Young Room in Old Main is named). There were two large farms on the estate, the West Farm and the Red Farm. The main residence was a large house, part of which had been built in the 1820s. Ultimately, this became the Headmaster's house. The buildings of the Red Farm would be adapted for use by the School, and plans were made for a gymnasium, playing fields, and four dormitories, each housing fifty girls and having apartment space for faculty.

On Saturday, May 2, 1959, a sunny, clear day, groundbreaking ceremonies for Kent's Girls Division took place. The officiant was the Right Reverend G. Ashton Oldham, formerly Bishop of Albany, and taking part in the rite asking God's blessing on the school were Cyrus R. Vance, vice-president of the board of trustees and chairman of the Vance Committee; Theodore Woodin, first selectman of the town of Kent; Lucien Fouke '59, senior prefect; the Reverend Kenneth W. Costin, Kent chaplain; and the Reverend John O. Patterson, rector and headmaster. The ceremony was attended by several hundred people—Skiff Mountain neighbors of the school, townspeople, trustees, alumni, faculty, students, and parents, and a number of girls applying for admission. Maxwell Moore '26, the architect for the project, and Theodore de F. Hobbs '30, the builder, were also present.

Above: Sidney Norwood Towle and John Oliver Patterson.

In the fall of 1959, Sidney Norwood Towle '31 was appointed associate headmaster and principal of the Girls Division of Kent School. Mr. Towle had entered Kent as a second former in September 1926, and he had distinguished himself as an athlete, captaining three teams and leading the varsity football team to an undefeated season. When he graduated, he was awarded Pater's Mug as the outstanding athlete. Father Sill described Mr. Towle as "one of the outstanding boys of the School in personality, in efficiency, in popularity, in loyalty, in religious life." He continued to pursue his athletic career at Yale, where he majored in English. In 1959, *Sports Illustrated* chose him as one of 25 former football stars who had distinguished themselves in the years since they had played. Upon his graduation from Yale in 1935, Father Sill offered Mr. Towle a job at Kent, but he had already decided upon a career in law, and he graduated from the Yale Law School in 1938. He served in the U.S. Army in World War II. After the war, he returned to Massachusetts to practice law in Boston. He became president of the alumni association in 1949 and 1950 and a member of the board of trustees. A member of the Vance Committee, he led the financial campaign for the Girls Division. He and his wife, Nancy, and their four children would take up residence in the Rawson House on the girls campus on October 1, 1959. Soon faculty appointments were announced, one of the first being that of the Reverend Willoughby Newton as chaplain and teacher of English and theology.

Below: The dedication of the library on the Hill.

On Tuesday, March 29, 1960, the Most Reverend Arthur Lichtenberger, Presiding Bishop of the Episcopal Church, officiated at the Service of Dedication of the Girls School (no longer simply the girls division!) in the library of the Red Barn.

Six months later, on September 11, 1960, the Girls School opened with an enrollment of 100 girls in the third and fourth forms. Two years later, when Father Patterson resigned, the board of trustees selected Sidney N. Towle to become Kent's fifth headmaster.

Right: The Girls School library.

Marcia Kline Sharp '63, the first senior prefect of the Girls School, wrote about the early days on Skiff Mountain in an article published in the *Quarterly* in 1983.

Below: Sidney N. Towle.

> We all knew, before we started at the Girls School, that there would be just a ninth and tenth grade—or third and fourth form as we were to call them—and no upper forms. We all knew we would be living in a brand new campus about five miles up Skiff Mountain Road from Kent's existing boys' campus. We all knew, because we had reviewed our Barn Shop samples, we would have a 'wardrobe' of clothes, executed almost entirely in blue and gray and including the 'Kent School plaid' skirt. And probably all knew there was something important and exciting about this venture, because Kent was the first—by a good five or ten years—of the great prestigious boys' schools to open its doors to girls.
>
> But there were still many surprises because what actually confronted us, that morning in September of 1960, was a fascinating scramble of things known and unknown. The things that most directly determined the nature of a fifteen-year-old's existence were perfectly clear and known—with nothing to suggest that this was the first day ever of a new institution. We learned that we would get up at 6:30 and be in bed with our lights out at 9:30. We learned that we already had a full range of student leaders, ready to go on day one, and including such things as a verger, a sacristan, and a dining hall steward. And we learned much more: there were classes every day but Sunday, Chapel every day, and a time set aside every day for doing our jobs and for going to Job Assembly. We did not drink coffee or have food in our rooms; we did not go into town or

have weekends. We would have stat store cards for necessary supplies, and discretionary funds of eighty cents a week (all in dimes.) We took five courses each, including English and theology. We were all on a 'team,' and the teams were Algos, Macedonians, Housatonics. We all lived in either dorm A, presided over by the Handfords, or dorm B, presided over by Father Newton and his Skye terrier, Sis. We were allowed to have record players on Wednesday and Saturday afternoons, after which time they were to be returned to the storeroom. We all ate three non-optional meals a day in our new dining hall. Mr. Towle sat in the middle of the long head table, facing out; the prefect sat at the left end and the faculty member on duty at the right end. The grace was posted on a little wooden board that sat down near the prefect end of the table.

  All these things had obviously been worked out in very orderly fashion in advance of that September morning. They communicated, quite clearly, that there already was a something called Kent Girls School, and that we one hundred third and fourth formers were simply coming to it, in the same way that all new students confront their schools.

  And yet, of course, we weren't simply coming as other students come. When you stopped to think about it, there were some big differences. There were, for example, no legends in our

Above: Robert H. Mattoon.

institutional life that fall—no come-from-behind sports coups from previous years; no places in the dorms that marked the spots where great boarding school mischief had been perpetrated; no identification of the Schoolhouse sprinkler system with the now famous exploits of 'Nancy Light and Tania Too'; no pictures of last year's student leaders—either looking foolish while somebody was pouring Cokes over their heads in the common room, or looking official in gray suits and black pumps.

　　　And there was no lore. No one knew, and thus no one told anyone else, that O.B. Davis would march into his classroom, take his books out of his green bag and place them neatly, in a single stack on his desk, with FAT RED on the bottom, and then strike terror into all of us by saying, 'Seize a piece of paper.' No one knew that Father Newton's theology stemmed almost entirely from Dostoyevsky rather than Matthew, Mark, Luke, and John. No one knew that the most official and anxiety-producing communication at Kent Girls School was a small white piece of memo paper, posted on the Schoolhouse bulletin board, on which was typed in all caps "PLEASE SEE ME AT YOUR EARLIEST CONVENIENCE. SNT." No one knew, exactly, what would happen if a lot of people smoked a lot of cigarettes in the boiler room. No one knew what would happen if it snowed the day we were supposed to go home for Christmas vacation. And no one knew that the only way to reach the outside world before a vacation was by Bluebird, on which two things always happened: a Prefect got on and called the roll, by memory Andersen, Barnum, Begle, Byrd, Brodhead, Claghorn, all the way through Wood and Woollard; and then someone struck up 'He's got Chi Chi and Tiny in his hands…he's got the whole world in his hands.'

　　　But with or without lore and legend, there was plenty to do that first year, plenty to learn about and respond to.

　　　From day one, we met a faculty that was clearly something special, even from the rather limited perspective students have on these things. There were a few who came up from the Boys School in those first few years—Mr. Davis to teach English, Mr. DeVillafranca and Mr. Bredberg in science, Mr. Mattoon for Russian. They gave us our exposure both to Kent as it had always been and to the quintessential New England Schoolmaster. And then there was the 'real' faculty, the ones who lived at the Girls School, who had made the same commitment to something new that we had. Consciously or not (but I can only suppose consciously) Kent had gone quite outside the New England prep school mainstream for most of the teaching positions at the Girls School. They gave us women like Miss Gassett, Miss Olmsted, and Miss Dunn … intense galvanizing women, teachers whose careers had been spent in public schools, teachers who surely must have found Kent Girls School as surprising as we did, and who seemed to have been recruited for the purpose of knocking intensity and commitment, as well as a love of learning, into our privileged heads. They gave us Mr. Handford, retired from Lancing College, one of England's fine boys' public schools, who— in spite of the fact that he had probably never taught girls in his life—seemed to stand for all possible wisdom and experience about how a new school for girls should really work. He had other talents too: translating Winnie the Pooh into Latin as a way to entice the less inspired; designing a masterfully simple system for rotating the work jobs, and ensuring that everyone got her fair share at morning dish crew. (I never had Mr. Handford as a teacher at Kent, but I have always remembered how helpful he was the year after I left Kent and went to Winchester, England, as an English-Speaking Union exchange student, and he left to return to England as well. I was

finding my English school something between bizarre and trying; he sent me a sympathetic letter which essentially boiled down to this message, 'You will find that people who live in other countries generally know best how to make them work.') And they gave us Father Newton, the gregarious chaplain—the only one of the Boys School faculty who had made the change to our school—who managed, all at once, to be mothered by us, to be the object of our schoolgirl crushes, to be the principal confessor, and to be our taskmaster at Biblical studies.

We also, in that first year, were called upon to meet this thing called coordination. In those days, it was not remotely synonymous with co-education. A few students went 'down' for art history in my fifth form year, but I, like most of my fellow students, never had a class at the Boys School. Nor did boys come to our classes. There was no informal or unscheduled traffic up and down the hill, and serious penalties ensued for disregarding that status quo. Formal opportunities for exchange did, however, exist. We went down, periodically and obligatorily, for Sunday Chapel (we had to get up earlier; the incense was stronger; the crumbcakes were less good than those produced in our dining hall; and the benches in the dining hall ran our stockings). We went down, periodically and voluntarily, for Saturday night movies and sports events. Letters came and went, and for many of us, the telephone booth vigil was a major element of Girls School life. But this was still, in the early '60s, the era of dates and pairs rather than friends and groups. One didn't just 'intermingle' casually, and thus there were large numbers of girls in the first few years who had a Kent School experience very little touched by the school in the valley.

And of course, we also did our best to lay down what would be the lore of the future. We made Ethel Walker's and Miss Porter's into our Loomis and our Taft, and we worked ourselves up to a fever pitch, three times a year, to try to beat those lean, tanned, incredibly athletic girls with purple and yellow ribbons. (It took four years at least, so the charter class never laid down that bit of lore.)

We experimented with anything that could be done to bring variety and individual expression into the uniforms. Dresses and blouses went on backwards; blouses went inexplicably

*Right: The uniform, "the uni,"
provided a number of options for the
girls, depending on the occasion.*

under dresses. Skirts went up to mid-thigh or down to mid-calf; color combinations as bizarre as could be made with Barn Shop colors (not very) flourished briefly. But none of this ever lasted too long: a fiat would appear on the bulletin board, and go out through the prefect system: "*ALL UNIFORM DRESSES AND BLOUSES WILL BE WORN FRONT WARDS ONLY. THIS SUPERCEDES ALL PRIOR BULLETINS ON THE SUBJECT.*"

We created the Kentettes, a small singing group—which was certainly derivative of the Kentones—and then the Sophistications, derivative of nothing except the lively irreverent atmosphere of Skiff Mountain.

And a few of us worked to adopt the Numeral Rock tradition to our situation. In early spring of 1963, the other three prefects and I had located a pile of old lumber in the shed next to the art building and behind the schoolhouse. I wrote to my father and requested that a jigsaw, some black paint, a brush, and a couple of handfuls of nails be mailed to me. When the packages arrived, we built and painted the numbers, each about eight feet high, at odd times during the weekends. And then—with delicious disregard for the full integrity of the prefect system in the dorms—we installed them on the roof of the gym by leaving our rooms about 11:00 one night (through the window screens), eluding the fairly sluggish night watchman, and making our way first to the shed, where the ladder and numerals were stored, and then to the gym, where we hoisted them up and installed them with great silent giggles and a feeling of tremendous daring. It was a fine moment when everyone woke up the next day, and I was saddened to learn that in later years the number construction had been regularized—and ostensibly improved—by having the

Left: The five prefects of the Class of '65 in their sixth form blazers, with the underform members of the Student Council.

maintenance staff do the building.

   The members of the classes of '63 and '64 are now separated from all of this by twenty years ... twenty years in which we have made our own personal decisions about colleges, about jobs, about families and children. Twenty years in which there has been as much change in women's lives as there had been in previous hundreds of years. Twenty years in which we, as a society, have learned an enormous amount about the education of girls and women. I find it fascinating—and

Left: Mrs. Towle served tea to the girls in the Headmaster's Residence on the Hill.

complicated—to look back at those early days, to sort them all out in my mind, and to come to any fixed reading of what it meant to all of us to be the pioneers. One thing I am increasingly certain of is this: that the circumstances of our founding put us in a strange 'no-man's land.' We were clearly not, in 1960-61, a girls school. There was, in fact, nothing feminine, nothing girlish, about our environment. We had no daisy chains, no Maypole celebrations, no big sisters, no cocoa and cookie rituals on Saturday nights. We had no 'feminine' spaces—no common rooms with rugs and soft chintz-covered sofas, nothing that looked the way it looked at Ethel Walker's. We had no songs about ribbons in the hair, no hovering elderly female presences to pour tea at our post-game receptions. We had no archaic graduation prizes for manners or deportment or grace. We wore skirts and blazers to Commencement, not white dresses and flowers.

More profoundly, we had no previous graduates of our school to have gone before us . . . to go to college, get jobs, have families, and show us what Kent girls grew up to be. We had no pictures of female founders and benefactors of our school. We had no Miss Hall, no Emma Willard, no Miss Porter in our past—only a Father Sill. So if you longed for those traditional girls school things—and there were those who did—you were probably undernourished at Kent.

And yet, in those early days, we were clearly not Kent either—not the real Kent. Neither James Gould Cozzens nor Cyrus Vance had gone to our Kent. The Spoon game was not our Armageddon; the morning sun never rent the haze on any Mount Algo that we could see. The hallowed places of Kent—Pater's Study, Numeral Rock, the boathouse—were all places where we had never been. The most admired students of Kent—who rowed at Henley, went to Yale, and perhaps ended up in the Episcopal ministry—were students we could never, in 1963, aspire to be. We simply couldn't have an image of our successful selves in the mainstream Kent tradition.

Instead we were, in those early years before the institutional reality had even begun to change, truly betwixt and between. Neither girls school, with its reward system, nor Kent School, with its. And my instinct is that Kent was underprepared for its girls, and underprepared for the kind of institutional affirmation it would have to make on their behalf. But I am also increasingly certain that there was something about those early years which made it worth it to be in no-man's land.

In many ways (although the words have probably never before been applied to Kent) Kent Girls School in 1960 had a lot of the elements of a feminist dream. We, particularly in the class of '63, went to Kent to build and run an institution. Kent's concept of student leadership, in combination with the newness of our school, meant that we had an inordinately large role in shaping what the Girls School was to become. Most of its norms and values—about student leadership, about the jobs program, about school spirit and what it meant and how one fit into it, about 'hazing' and seniority, about cheating or not, about even fuzzier things like what kinds of students were affirmed by peers and faculty alike—came from us. Whether those norms lasted (they probably have changed as much as the rest of the society) and whether those norms were, in an absolute sense, 'good' (probably they all were not) is not terribly important. What is important is that our two founding classes had the rare chance to speak and to act with a clear slate, and to know that important people were watching and caring about what we did.

And so, unfettered by a more conventional girls school tradition, we did not have to overcome the daisy chains and ribbons to dream a bold future for ourselves and our school. And, relatively insulated from the Boys School in all but name, we did not have to spend the early years of coordination fighting either the tokenism or the second class citizen status that virtually all girls

and women have found when they have been the first ones to 'co-educate' an all male institution.

You could say, I suppose, that Kent Girls School was, by most girls schools' standards, a little rough and ragged, and a little light on the graces. I'm sure many of our mothers thought that. But it was ours, as true and important a piece of turf as many of us in the class of '63 will ever see again. Far too seldom in our society do girls get to play at institutional development in an important context. And the Girls School gave us that.

Ann Dickinson remembers that "There was a culture of singing, whether in chapel or glee club. So many of us joined together in singing even in informal settings." Alumnae from those early days remember singing "The Strife is O'er" on the Headmaster's lawn (though some recall this a bit differently, remembering singing it in the Dining Hall) at the end of exams. Traditions were born: "We were part of a larger, older school but we were apart on a mountaintop. To go anywhere we had to pile on the Bluebird bus for a sometimes hair-raising trip down the mountain. We were part of a boys school but this was not coeducation but 'coordinate' education. We girls had the sense that we were making new traditions every day. Ethel the elephant, for instance, emerged from an oil stain on the asphalt on the Oval." The ring ceremony became the means of passing on the new traditions, of making the transition from being a fifth former to being a sixth former, a leader of the School, a formal and memorable experience. "Everyone remembers her first job. . . . There was a sense of pride in doing our jobs and feeling that we were responsible for the well-being of the School. There were dark whisperings of schools where there were maids who made up girls' beds. . . . Some of us chafed against the rules more than others. . . . But there was a rhythm to each day and each week that united us all. Even when you hated the schedule and the rules, there was a part of you that acknowledged some relief at having structure to direct you.

"Each and every one of us remembers vividly a few teachers who changed us in some way, whether by exceptional teaching or providing emotional support and guidance." Some of the men and women, not mentioned earlier, who are remembered as being "stand-out teachers" are Gwen Heuss, Lyn Olmstead, and Esther Gassett.

Thirty-two years later, at the Service of Remembrance and Thanksgiving on June 13, 1992, which officially marked the closing of the Hill campus, Esther Gassett Olivey spoke of the "Thirty-two Years of Excellence" that were coming to a close on the Hill, to continue in the Valley. She began by paying tribute to "those who had laid the groundwork for the opening on September 10, 1960. Much tribute needs to be given to Sidney and Nancy Towle, Bill and Jeanne

Below: Esther Gassett.

Right: Handford and Case Dorms on the Hill Campus.

Howard, Alex and Sally Uhle, and Basil and Betty Handford and others. . . . Also I would like to call attention to the tried and true veterans from the Boys School who taught one or more classes at the Girls School. These were O.B. Davis in English, Coe deVillafranca and Hal Bredberg in science, and Benny Mattoon in languages. With these illustrious people and the standards of the Boys School to guide us, we accepted the challenge. . . . Foremost in my mind is the raised level of learning that was often developed in the classroom. This intangible product sometimes referred to as 'love of learning' was often produced by fertile young minds coached and guided by enthusiastic and dedicated faculty, many of whom were scholars in their field. They welcomed new ideas and were interested in the wonders of science, mathematics, social studies, languages, the arts, music, and drama. Kent has provided a healthy opportunity for students and their mentors to live, work, play, and attend classes in an atmosphere where ideas are welcomed with respect and encouragement."

Needless to say, there was a building boom on Skiff Mountain in the four years between the purchase of the Rawson Farm and the day the first girl graduated from Kent. Farm buildings were transformed into the Hill Schoolhouse; a corn crib was transformed into an art studio, and where chickens had once saluted the dawn with clucks and crows, Kent musicians now made a different kind of music. Dormitories—the first known as Dorm D and later dedicated to Julia Kingborn McGovern— were built. In the next three years three more dormitories were named: Handford in April 1965, Case in February 1966, and Springs in February 1967. In the summer of 1962 the infirmary for the Girls Campus was completed, and the following spring the auditorium-gymnasium was

Below: The Girls School, with the oratory in the lower right of the picture.

ESTHER GASSETT

Esther Gassett came to Kent in 1960 to teach at the newly founded Girls School on Skiff Mountain. There she made her presence felt, not only because she was a superb math teacher and a demanding dorm master, but also because she filled the halls of Case Dorm with the fragrance of homemade pies and cookies. Over forty-five years later her former students and colleagues still remember her with a combination of awe and love.

After a long career in public education, Miss Gassett came to Kent from Oklahoma, where she had been chosen "math teacher of the year" by the Oklahoma Society of Professional Engineers. Elected to Phi Beta Kappa for her outstanding teaching, she was, in the words of Henry Syer, her chairman when she came to Kent, "one of the best classroom teachers [he had] ever seen."

After the launching of Sputnik, the National Science Foundation was given the task of upgrading the teaching of science and mathematics in American secondary schools. Two teachers were chosen from each state to rethink the teaching of mathematics, one of them Esther Gassett. She went to Yale in the summer of 1958 as part of the School Mathematics Study Group charged with the task of getting us into the space race. Thirteen years later, one of her students, astronaut Stewart Roosa, piloted Apollo XIV around the moon. In the celebration after the flight, he publicly acknowledged the great debt he owed to his teacher, Miss Gassett (*Kent Quarterly* Winter 1995).

At Kent, Miss Gassett is still remembered by those she taught who went on to walk — or try to walk — in her footsteps. They remember her skill as a teacher, her "fierce determination to teach anyone anything as long as he or she was willing to try," her patience, her loyalty, her generosity.

DEDICATIONS

1964 YEARBOOK DEDICATION

Whole-heartedly dedicated to her profession and deeply concerned for the girls of Kent, though at times she scares us half to death, she holds our complete faith and trust. Never ceasing her justified gripes about "sloppy" attitudes and "peanut-brained" students — never impatient to spend hours on end teaching a single willing individual. Always putting us in our place — always willing to listen to our problems and to give sympathy where it was due. An amazing character she is with her stern will and unselfish heart. We can never forget her — we hope that we shall never forget her advice.

In appreciation for all that she has given to us, we the girls of Kent School would like to dedicate the *1964 KENT* to Miss Esther Gassett.

The 1964 yearbook dedication to Esther Gassett.

Perhaps her own words provide the best way to remember her: "It doesn't matter what happens to me, or you, but the things we stand for, the things we believe in, the things that breed through our consciousness, our very life blood, our thread of living is preserved somewhere. It has nothing to do with our bodies. I get a real kick out of the idea that as long as there are 500 kids alive that I taught that something I taught them may be doing some good. I get a sense of continuity there" (*Kent Quarterly* Fall 2004/Winter 2005).

Above: (Top) The dedication of the Manuel D. Nadal Hockey Rink in 1966. (Bottom) A recent picture of the Springs Center, which includes the Nadal Hockey Rink.

Right: 1964 varsity hockey.

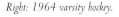

dedicated in honor of Mr. and Mrs. Byron S. Miller, and St. Mark's Chapel, located in that building, was dedicated.

Because the chapel was located in the gymnasium, there was a need for a place which could be used solely for religious purposes, a quiet place where a girl might go to pray or simply be alone to think. On November 19, 1963, the Oratory at the Girls School was consecrated by Bishop Gray of Connecticut, assisted by the Reverend Dr. John Heuss, rector of Trinity Church in New York City. It was given in memory of Father Sill by the parish of Trinity Church. Father Sill's father, the Reverend Thomas Henry Sill, the Curate of Trinity Chapel at 26th Street in New York City, had established St. Chrysostom's Chapel at the corner of 34th Street and 7th Avenue in New York, and during his years at Columbia and General Theological Seminary, Father Sill had been active at St. Chrysostom's, working with the boys in the parish.

While growth and change were going on 4.5 miles up Skiff Mountain, and while the boys in the valley were getting used to the idea of there being girls up there in a school called Kent, there were changes in the valley, too. In January 1966 a new, covered hockey rink was dedicated to Manuel D. Nadal '17, Kent's long-time hockey coach.

That was followed in February by the dedication of the new squash courts, the Charles E. (Tod) Brainard Squash Racquets Courts. Tod Brainard '26 had introduced squash to Kent, and he, his family, and several other Kent alumni made the building of the courts possible. Elsewhere on the Valley campus momentous changes in the 'look' of Kent were occurring, for just

MANUEL DAVETT NADAL '17

"Bill" Nadal entered Kent in 1911 and began an association with the School that would last until his death at the age of 80. He was an outstanding athlete, earning twelve varsity letters, and he was the senior prefect of the Class of 1917. At the time, he held records for touchdowns and total yardage in football, and he was captain of the baseball and hockey teams. After graduating, he served in the Marine Corps for two years. He then returned to Kent, where he served as assistant headmaster to Father Sill, director of admissions, and athletic director. He coached baseball, football, and hockey. The last team Bill Nadal coached, the 1958-1959 hockey team, was undefeated and untied. In the sixty-five years he was an integral part of Kent, he saw the School grow from 72 boys to 600 boys and girls in 1977. Among the more than 4,000 students he coached in those years were Cyrus Vance and Sydney Towle. In a final tribute to Bill Nadal when he died in May 1977, William Armstrong said, "Mr. Nadal was my senior and my superior. As a young Master I tried to copy his devotion to Kent and his sense of duty. As I grew older I came to know the impossibility of that goal. Seeing and knowing him one came to agree with the poet who said that if a man is strong and gentle too, 'even the blind can see his qualities'" (excerpted from *The Kent News*, October 1, 1977).

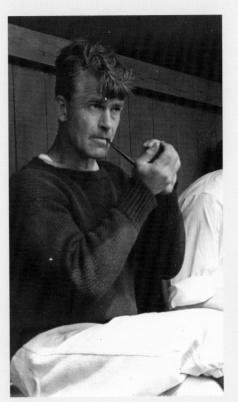

Manuel D. Nadal '17.

north of North Dorm a new Science Center was being built. Groundbreaking ceremonies were held on November 6, 1965, and on October 22, 1966, the new building was dedicated in honor of Fairleigh S. Dickinson, Jr. The campus on the banks of the Housatonic was growing.

On the Hill, the indoor riding ring at the stables was completed in 1968, and on Prize Day, June 3, 1971, the library on the Boys campus was dedicated in honor of John G. Park '28. "Bronx" Park had worked tirelessly to make Kent's library worthy of the School, and to this day the library, now in Schoolhouse, bears his name. Later that year, the Field House and Tennis House were named in honor of Robert A. Magowan '23.

It was also under Headmaster Towle's leadership that the International Baccalaureate Program was established in October 1979 as a way of attracting foreign students to Kent and strengthening the academic program. Kent was the first major independent school in the United States to start such a program.

Above: The Magowan Field House.

Below: Taking the Bluebird.

There were other changes, too. Gradually the two schools, separate but equal, came closer, as boys and girls began to take more courses on each other's campus. Advanced Placement courses and art history were co-ed by the 1962-1963 academic year. At that point, students would get rides up or down the hill with faculty members who were heading that way for a class. It wasn't long before the numbers began to increase and more boys and girls were making the trip. Schedules had to be arranged so that this could take place with a minimum of difficulty—though those who lived through those years remember how hard this was to achieve. And eventually the Bluebird buses were making regular trips up and down Skiff Mountain Road, and classes were, essentially, coeducational. No longer was Saturday night the only night of the week when boys and girls mingled. There were difficulties, especially in the winter, when a snowstorm could disrupt the system mightily. Boys and girls were hurried back to their respective campuses before the road became dangerous, classes for the rest of the day might be half full, and if the storm became intense, faculty members, too, hastened up—or down—the hill, causing the occasional cancellation of a class.

When the Towle years are remembered, it is wise to remember also that for the country these were years of great turbulence, and leading a school during that time could not have been easy—or simple. In 1960, John Fitzgerald Kennedy, a charismatic young senator from Massachusetts, had been elected president of the United States, taking office in perilous times. The Russian Bear was flexing its muscles, and in the fall of 1962, as Russian ships steamed toward Cuba, war seemed imminent. Fortunately those ships turned back, and, for a few brief months it seemed as if all would be well. Then on that dreadful day in November 1963, Kennedy was assassinated in Dallas, Texas, and the country was plunged into mourning. Lyndon Johnson became president, with his dreams of a Great Society in which all men and women would receive equal treatment. All would be well – except that at the same time the United States was becoming more and more deeply embroiled in the war in Viet Nam. Then more assassinations followed: Robert F. Kennedy in 1967 and Martin Luther King, Jr. in 1968, both of them carrying the burdens of leadership in turbulent times. Riots erupted on campuses and in cities. Students were killed at Kent State, and news of the massacre at My Lai appalled the world. Protests against the war made headlines. All was not well.

And in these difficult times, Sidney Towle had the equally difficult job of leading a school. The unrest in the nation was felt everywhere, even in schools like Kent. *The Kent News*, which, surprisingly in earlier years had made almost no mention of the Great Depression and, more recently, had made no mention of JFK's assassination, reflected this unrest with discussions of the war, polls about the war, the draft, and school rules. The almost worshipful attitude toward Kent seen in the newspaper in earlier years was replaced by criticism. Occasionally Mr. Towle would try to diffuse tensions brought to the campus from events outside it by declaring a holiday in conjunction with some global occasion, such as the first Earth Day.

So Mr. Towle's years as headmaster were not easy ones, though they were fruitful ones for the School.

Sidney Towle died at his home on Skiff Mountain on November 5, 1980, after a long illness. At his funeral in St. Joseph's Chapel, O.B. Davis gave the eulogy. He said, "I remember . . . the grace and courtesy with which he met troubles and problems from the beginning of his tenure at Kent until the very end. He was a man . . . of very strong conviction and with strong feelings to give that conviction steam. Like Father Sill, Mr. Towle hated to lose. He hated to lose when he played tennis, he hated to lose with Kent teams, he hated the idea of losing arguments. (I say the idea because he did not lose many arguments around here during the twenty years I knew him). . . . With people he did not like he was scrupulously and painfully just; and he was scrupulously and painfully just with people he did like. On rare occasions, confronted by opposition, Sidney Towle did lose a formidable temper, but the courteous apology he would make later was well worth the trauma of that event.

"I remember Sidney Towle's devotion to a conception of duty and justice based on the welfare of Kent School. When that welfare was at issue he would not spare others and he certainly would not spare himself. . . . I remember our Headmaster's administrative judgment. . . Mr. Towle effected at Kent a gradual change for which he was sometimes criticized. From being a school at which every 'operating' decision was the immediate business of the Headmaster, we became a school at which such decisions were made by appropriate deans, directors, and chairmen. The ultimate responsibility which the Headmaster did not and could not relinquish was that of demanding results for Kent School from his subordinate officers. . . .

"Finally I remember that he was my friend, loyal and just to me. I remember a genial, knowledgeable, magnanimous Christian gentleman. I remember a devoted father and husband. I remember no malice but plenty of fight. I remember some errors, but nothing mean" (Excerpted from *The Kent News*, November 15, 1980).

NANCY ROBERTS TOWLE

One of Sidney Towle's assets, first as principal of the Girls School and then as headmaster of Kent, was his wife, Nancy. Together they worked tirelessly to see that the School prospered. But Nancy had her own special gift for Kent. She was quick to see the potential Skiff Mountain's open acres and forested trails held for offering excitement, challenge, and discipline to girls through the sport of riding. For two decades, starting with four horses and a cow barn, she pursued her lifelong avocation by creating the Riding Program and developing it to the point where it enjoyed both a national and international reputation, "virtually without peer among riding programs at academic schools and colleges" (*Kent News*, May 1982). "She demanded quality and the best that one could give, and any student who showed an interest in horses was given the opportunity to participate at all levels of ability" (Kent T. Kay, veterinarian). In his tribute to Nancy when she died, John S. Kerr quoted her son, Lex, and Esther Gassett. Both remembered Nancy's being a gourmet cook and a gardener skilled at creating beauty in her gardens at Kent and at her home by the sea in Ipswich. But even more, they remembered her loyalty, her sense of humor, and her love of life. Esther Gassett said, "She was a survivor in life, and her spirit will prevail." (excerpted from the article by John S. Kerr, *Kent Quarterly*, Spring 1993)

Sidney and Nancy Towle.

Riding in 1960.

And so, seventy-four years after its founding, Kent again faced the challenge of finding the right person to lead it into its next chapter, one that would prove momentous in the changes it would bring to the School. During the interim between Sidney Towle's death and the appointment of the next headmaster, Hart Perry, who was Dean of Boys as well as coach of the KSBC, served on the Interim Operating Committee. For all practical purposes he managed the day-to-day operations of the School, reporting to Board President Peter Conze '38.

In a letter to Samuel Bartlett, who had left Kent to found South Kent, Father Sill wrote that a good headmaster "must be in the thick of things from the start." An article in the *News* of February 14, 1981, said, "[I]t is evident that Sill believed fully in a headmaster who would not only set an example for the students but who would make an effort to be involved with them in their daily life. The admiration those who knew Father Sill had for him testifies to the success of his methods; the ideas of a man who was able to start a successful school with 'two hundred dollars in cash and a few pledges' should, perhaps, be considered in Kent's search for a new head" ("Finding a headmaster, founding a school," Betsy Sutherland, *Kent News*, February 14, 1981).

In the fall of 1965 a boy from the Chicago area had entered Kent as a third former, a third former who wasn't quite sure he wanted to stay. But stay he did, taking a leadership role in the School and becoming Senior Prefect of the Class of 1969, captain of the tennis team, winner of the Morehead Scholarship, and voted "Most likely to succeed" by his class. In the fall of 1969, he became Kent's youngest trustee ever to serve on the Board and was appointed to the Trustees' Academic Committee. Following his graduation from Harvard, *magna cum laude*, with a *summa cum laude* honors thesis in American history, he went on to Yale Divinity School, where he received his master's degree. He then became a parish priest in Lake Forest, Illinois. In the fall of 1980, Richardson Whitfield Schell '69 became Kent's chaplain and head of the theology department, and on July 1, 1981, he became Kent School's sixth headmaster, with his formal institution as headmaster on November 12, 1981, in a service which commemorated not only his becoming headmaster and rector but also the 75th anniversary of the founding of Kent School.

Above: The Very Reverend Lawrence Rose, Dean of General Theological Seminary, Subchancellor of Kent in the '60s.

In 1981, the Reverend Polly Kasey was appointed chaplain, the first woman to hold this position at Kent. In 1983, buildings in the Valley and on the Hill were renovated, perhaps contributing to the movement toward consolidation. North Dorm and Schoolhouse Dorm in the Valley had work done on them, and an addition to the Hill Schoolhouse was underway. A computer course was added to the curriculum, and in 1983 Elizabeth Klein received the first IB diploma. Cable TV arrived, and in 1985 PCs for student use were placed in the Schoolhouse and the computer room on the Hill. Old Main became the Admissions Building. In 1985, the Founder's League was formed, expanding the athletic leagues in which Kent held membership. In 1987 Kent had its own permanent radio station for the first time, broadcasting to the campus. Permanent, because earlier in 1970 or so, John Hinners had collected about a half dozen boys, taken them to New York to get the FCC licenses and constructed a small 5-watt studio in the Schoolhouse. The station played a lot "smooth rock" and folk, and the on-air talent was dominated by Rick Rinehart '72 and his roommate, Ric Burwell '72. A moment of levity, however, brought the enterprise to a hasty conclusion, leaving Kent without its own station until 1987. Curriculum changes continued: Chinese was offered on the Hill.

In the 1980s Kent suffered losses, too, as the School mourned the deaths of Father Chalmers in January 1981, Lee Gilliam in October 1984, Roger Sessions '11 in April 1985, the Reverend Lawrence Rose '19 in October 1987, Father Patterson in November 1988, and Henry Syer in April 1989.

Slowly but surely, Kent was changing, but as it did so, it would remain the School that Father Sill had dreamt into existence eighty years earlier.

OCTOBER BELONGS TO GOD

William H. Armstrong

ONE DAY WITH INSTANT DARK AND DAWN, or one night with dreams racing backward, when I have laid me down at my time's meager pace run full, on some mist-blurred mountain or in some valley grayed by my mind's anxious gloom, my Creator will ask of me a question. I gave you my glorious creation to enjoy. What did you do with it? Did you lift up your eyes unto the hills? If that is the question, then why did you make me too small for the answer, God?

Puny of heart and with vision so small—I am incapable of the beauty you have spread upon Mt. Algo and Skiff Mountain—your patterns of crimson and gold—your poetry set to music on the rhythm of the wind, a hymn to harvest and rest, a certain declaration to transfiguration and resurrection. A thousand rainbows unrolled, cut up into patches, like Band-Aids to cover all the scars of earth-man's blemishes.

A child romps in a pile of your gold in some dooryard and laughs.

My heart is too small to contain such glory—my vision too narrow and bleak.

I walk on your rainbow carpet of maple and sumac and shadblow, searching in vain for a new direction along some old familiar road—hearing your living silence—your living silence from which I would learn. Who but you would hear me if I cry?

Then why, God, with puny heart and vision so small, did you give me a soul so big—to long for your measureless beauty in earth—that longing forever unfilled? Better contentment would be mine to crawl in the dark corridors of dust with the blind mole—to live in a cave with the bat, hanging from a dark damp rock, never seeing your sun and earth, feeling my way on your night wind. Or live in the depths of black waters—mapping my course with scaly eyeless creatures of the deep. Or be down in the mines with some Caliban—in the bowels of a sulking black earth—with a lamp in my cap for a star.

Only for these is my heart and my vision adequate. But you've laid out a path of gold. Then why do I stumble in fear and plod so grudgingly?

In your Book I have found the words: "The harvest has passed, the summer is ended, and we are not saved."

"Blessed is the man who walks not with the ungodly, nor stands in the circle of sinners, nor sits in the seat of the scornful—for he shall be as a tree planted by the rivers of waters that brings forth its fruit in its season."

There too I have found your word: "Cursed be the man who trusts in man—for he shall be as a thorn-bush in the desert, and shall see no beauty when it comes."

And in your Book too I have read: "The fig tree knoweth her season." Because of my puny heart, oh God, I am confounded by seasons—and one runs upon another before I have measured it, and it is wasted before I know its signs.

Why? Why do you not speak to me, God, as you spoke to David at Rephaim: "Let it be," you said on the night breeze, "When you hear the sound of the wind in the tops of the mulberry trees, then shall you bestir yourself, for then shall the Lord go out before you."

This once, Lord, this October, on Mt. Algo or on Skiff Mountain or by the Housatonic, speak to me, and tell me my glass-darkly eyes are open, and my puny heart enlarged, that I may know the mystery of one of your painted leaves—whirling down on your breath—turning, turning on the surface of Schoggen or Macedonia Brook on its way to the Housatonic, and a grave in some dark slough, from which, in Spring, it shall send up a may-fly full-winged. And of transfiguration this is all I shall ever ask—all I shall ever need to know.

And I read again from your Book. For you have said to me: "Go out with joy—and the mountains and the hills shall break forth before you in singing, and all the trees of the field shall clap their hands."

Surely, God, you must mean in October.

If you had created time—which you didn't—because you had no need for it, you only made the sun to rule the day, and the moon to rule the night. But if you had made time and had belittled yourself just a tiny bit to choose a month, a season—truly one special choice would have been October. Painting the hills running down to the Housatonic with your wide brush. Pouring great pails of flame-paint upon ten thousand generations of mountain oaks planted by careless squirrels who forgot where they had buried their acorns.

One thing only I ask, oh God. Enlarge my puny heart. Let me see as the child romping on a feathery mound of your October gold. Let me know this lovely place, this blessed time, this life—all stranger than a dream that makes the sleep of the laborer sweet.

This, God, that I may answer when I stand before you and you ask me the question: "I gave you my glorious creation to enjoy, what did you do with it?"

—Kent Quarterly, Fall 1984

CREW

SATURDAY, APRIL 15, 1922—A GIG MANNED BY TWO Kent students, Noye and J. Brewster, with Father Sill in the coxswain's seat, was launched in the Housatonic. It was an historic day for the School, for with this small beginning, the Kent School crew program began. According to the *Kent News*, April 21, 1922, it was not an especially auspicious beginning, for "one of the oars was adjusted wrong, and a strong current forced the craft down the stream at full speed. A part of the old bridge was lodged in the middle of the course, and it was practically impossible to avoid. A landing was effected, however, in such a way that little harm was done to the gig. Soon, Mr. Voorhees' motor boat appeared and [he] assisted in righting the gig and repairing the small damage done. After the boat had been launched again, it started off downstream. . . . At a point about two miles down the river, the boat was turned around with its nose upstream, and the arduous task of making headway against a very swift current began. Here the endurance of Noye and Brewster asserted itself, and it was not long before the exponents of the first crew in the history of Kent School rounded the bend in the river and swung into shore under the new boat house."

Father Sill must have dreamed about this day from the time he chose the site for his School. He had been the coxswain on the Columbia crew, which he had led to victory in the first Poughkeepsie Regatta ever held. As coach of Kent's crew, he set his first boys a regimen of setting-up exercises, work on the machines, and a mile run every afternoon. On the water, he worked with two boys at a time, convinced that he would develop a steadier crew than if he began at once with the eight-oared shells. Just days before this first foray down the river, the boats ordered had actually arrived at Kent: two gigs, a centipede, and two shells. There were four crews at first, Blue I and Blue II, Grey I and Grey II.

Brewster and Noye, the brave young men who ventured out in the gig, were seated number 7 and Stroke in Blue I. When interviewed by the *News*, Father Sill said, "By the end of the week, we expect to have two eights out on the river. Of course it must be taken into consideration that none of the fellows on the present crew have ever had any experience in a shell before. Judging from the way the fellows have worked on the machines, however, it will not take long before they will get familiar with conditions on the water. For a short time during the trial spin last Saturday, the rowing was rather awkward, but by the time the rowers got used to the shell they showed very good prospects, and were able to handle the gig in splendid fashion. Of course, we cannot expect to turn out a finished crew by June, but, through the start made this year, future crews will be developed with greater ease. As far as the actual material goes, we are well fitted out. The physical condition of the Blue first crew is all that can be desired. This crew averages over 160 pounds in weight, and is close to six feet in height.

"It is barely a month since we even started to think of having a crew this spring, and things have come along a great deal faster than I expected. The new boat house will prove adequate for our present equipment, and altogether, the prospects loom up as very bright."

In the years that followed, Kent developed crews that rowed against Yale and Harvard as well as form crews in all forms, second through sixth. And in 1927, Kent was the first American school crew to row at Henley when Coach Sill took his Eight there to enter the Thames Challenge Cup event. The School was especially blessed when Lord Rothermere gave Kent a new shell. While Kent had about 15 days of rowing before the regatta, Kent drew the Thames Rowing Club in the first heat, and was nosed out by only five feet in the fastest heat of the event.

1930: On board the Majestic.

Robert N. Ogden '27 reported on the race in the Henley Supplement of the *Kent News*, October 11, 1927.

The race the Kent crew was entered in, the Thames Challenge Cup, was the largest of all, there being twenty-eight entries. Of these a few were schools, some were college crews from Oxford or Cambridge, but the majority were rowing clubs. . . . At the drawing, which had taken place three days before the races, we were scheduled to row the second crew of the Thames Rowing Club. This club is a large organization of nearly two thousand members, most of whom have rowed in college and school boats and have continued their rowing after graduation.

Ogden's description of the race is quite detailed, well worth going back to, but it is the end of the race that is most impressive, considering that these Kent boys were rowing against a formidable crew. Kent was leading by ten feet at the quarter mile, and at the mile the two shells were even. Then, "one hundred yards from the finish, the Thames crew sprinted, and although Kent did their best to catch them, it was impossible to cut down the lead.

And so Thames won, beating us out in a magnificent finish by a scant quarter length. . . . We stayed in Henley for the rest of the Regatta and . . . saw the Thames first crew win the Grand [Challenge Cup], and the crew that beat us win the Thames Challenge Cup quite easily, and although it was, of course, a disappointment to be put out in the first race, still there was the consolation that we gave the winners a harder race than anyone else in the event."

In 1930, Kent again was Henley-bound. Lord Rothermere again presented Kent with a new Sims shell, which was ready for the crew at Henley. The oarsmen sailed for England on the *Majestic* on June 6th. On board ship Father Sill kept a tight rein on his crew, for once they arrived in England they would be taking college entrance exams. Every day they studied, tutored by the teacher-coaches who were sailing with them. On the Monday after they arrived in England they took their exams at the Henley Town Hall. Days later, the School rowed for the Thames trophy, won the previous year by the Browne and Nichols Crew. The crew enjoyed several successes, especially in the race against the Princeton

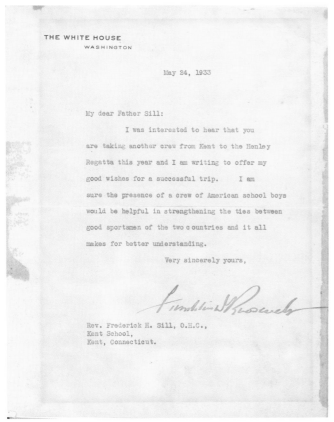

THE WHITE HOUSE
WASHINGTON

May 24, 1933

My dear Father Sill:

I was interested to hear that you
are taking another crew from Kent to the Henley
Regatta this year and I am writing to offer my
good wishes for a successful trip.   I am
sure the presence of a crew of American school boys
would be helpful in strengthening the ties between
good sportsmen of the two countries and it all
makes for better understanding.

Very sincerely yours,

Rev. Frederick H. Sill, O.H.C.,
Kent School,
Kent, Connecticut.

Letter from President Roosevelt, May 23, 1933.

hundred and fifty pound crew, which Kent won by half a length. But the race tired the boys, and so in their last race of the Regatta, against Worcester College, they lost, again by only a quarter of a length.

At the Prize Day exercises on Tuesday, June 6, 1933, the day before the Crew sailed for Henley on the *Berengaria*, Father Sill read a letter addressed to him from President Franklin D. Roosevelt. Father Sill had known President Roosevelt for many years, and entertained him at Kent in the summer of 1930 when, together with Governor Cross of Connecticut, he opened the Kent Fair.

My dear Father Sill:

I was interested to hear that you are taking another crew from Kent to the Henley Regatta this year and I am writing to offer my good wishes for a successful trip.

I am sure the presence of a crew of American school boys will be helpful in strengthening the ties between good sportsmen of the two countries, and it all makes for better understanding.

Very sincerely yours,
Franklin D. Roosevelt

Kent triumphed in its 1933 appearance at Henley when the crew won the Thames Challenge Cup, defeating the Bedford Rowing Club by two lengths. The British press was most enthusiastic about Kent's win. The rowing correspondent in *The Times* said "The standard of rowing was not below the average after all. Kent School were almost certainly the best crew that ever rowed in the Thames Cup" (*Kent News*, October 4, 1933).

On May 31, 1937, *Life* magazine had a feature article on Kent's crew. "When the third annual interscholastic regatta of the Schoolboy Rowing Association of America is held at Lake Quinsigamond, Worcester, Mass. May 29, many an excellent school, including old and famed St. George's will be represented. But from a rowing point of view, even the most swank and expensive of U.S. preparatory schools must yield to Connecticut's Kent, where expense is conditioned to the pupil's parent's purse and where swank is subordinated to the simple life. . . . Because Father Sill is an old crew man himself (1895 Columbia varsity), and because the Housatonic River is nearby, Kent crews have long been famous. In 1927 and 1930, Kent crews were the first boarding-school crews to row in the British Henley, a fixture which they won in 1933."

Again, in the June 28, 1948, issue of *Life*, Kent crew was featured, this time with Stuart Auchincloss '48 on the cover. Just the week before, fourteen boys had sailed for England to defend the Thames Challenge Cup, which Kent had won three times. *Life* reported, "What football means to Notre Dame, rowing means to Kent. . . . As soon as Father Sill could manage it, which was not until 1922, Kent had a crew. Today it has 11 crews, six coaches and 110 boys (out of an enrollment of 300) who go out for rowing."

In the years since, the Kent School Boat Club has rowed at Henley 32 times, winning five times, most recently in 1972 when they had an undefeated season at home and in the U.K., winning the Princess Elizabeth Cup at Henley. This undersized but overachieving crew helped celebrate the 50th anniversary of rowing at Kent by breaking three course records (Kent, Worcester, Stotesbury) and becoming the first Kent crew to be

1935 Henley Crew.

named national schoolboy champions. Appropriately, their shell was christened the Frederick Herbert Sill, and today hangs from the ceiling of the second floor of the Partridge Rowing Center.

The *Kent News* on October 13, 1973, had a page one headline: Girls Take Control of the Housatonic. A new era in Kent rowing had begun. "The oarswomen

Reprinted courtesy of Life Magazine.

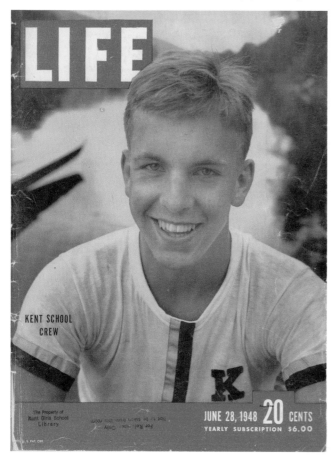

took to the Girls School pond Thursday, September 13, at 4:05 PM under the watchful eye of the President of the National Association of Amateur Oarsmen and Head Coach of Kent crew, W. Hart Perry, for indoctrination and tryouts." Mr. Perry announced that Girls crew was now a fully recognized fall sport and that he anticipated a four-week schedule against Yale, Middletown High School, Roosevelt High School, and competition at the Head-of-the-Charles Regatta. Twenty-one girls showed up for the first day of practice. After rowing on the pond for a few weeks, the girls finally made the trip down the hill to the Housatonic, rowing out of the old boathouse on Schaghticoke Road. Hart Perry asked Mark McWhinney '75, then in his fifth form year, to be his assistant coach, manager, and launch driver for the KGBC.

In 1981 Mr. McWhinney became the KGBC's head coach. By that time girls crew was a full-fledged varsity sport, but they were still competing in the fall. Highlights of that fall season included best-ever finishes at the Head of the Connecticut and Head of the Charles Regattas, and the second boat defeated Simsbury in a dual race on the Housatonic, the first time that a Kent girls boat beat Simsbury. It wasn't until the spring of 1983 that the girls began competing in what was considered to be "the real season for high school rowing." Up to that time, the girls had been competing in a boys' hull with boys' oars. Now they needed a new racing shell. One was ordered from Vespoli, and named the *Elizabeth Dickinson*, for Kent's first female trustee. After a busy

1950.

and very successful spring season, it was time for the New England Championships. The First Boat won the Kenneth Burns Bowl by 3.25 seconds, beating a strong St. Paul's boat. They were New England champions in their first attempt in only the tenth year of girls rowing at Kent. More successes followed, and the KGBC won the championship in four of the first five years it competed for it.

If competing at Henley was the highlight of the early years for the KSBC, competing at the National Championship in their fourth year of spring rowing was the highlight of the season for the 1986 KGBC. The next year, competing in a four borrowed from Rumsey Hall because some of the girls in the First Boat were unable to go the Nationals, Kent once again triumphed.

Consolidation of the campuses in 1992 added flexibility to the practice schedule and depth to the program as a third eight was added, but, in the words of Coach McWhinney, "what never changed during these years were the girls' pride, hard work, and dedication toward getting smoother, stronger, and faster."

From those beginnings grew the formidable Kent Girls Boat Club that continues to this day. In 2002, the Kent girls went to England for the first time and rowed to victory in both the Reading and Henley Women's Regattas. They returned in 2005, coming in second to a strong English crew. Today the Kent Girls Boat Club continues the tradition begun by the boys in 1922.

One thing about the success of Kent crew that is absolutely clear is that while it is about competing and winning, about discipline and physical courage, it is also about the men who have coached. From the beginning, when Father Sill launched that first gig in the Housatonic, Kent has been blessed with fine coaches. The most memorable at this hundred-year mark are Father Sill himself, T. Dixon Walker, and Hart Perry.

T. Dixon Walker '19 was born in 1900 and attended Kent until his fifth form year, when he, like others in his class, left to serve in the military. After attending Yale, he returned to Kent and worked as alumni secretary. He served as the assistant crew coach under Father Sill and was named Head Coach in 1937. In 1942 he again left Kent, this time to serve in World

1953.

1972.

The 1985 New England Champions with Coach McWhinney on the right.

T. Dixon Walker—Tote—in 1959.

War II. A whole book could be written about Tote Walker – and undoubtedly will be some day – but a few reminiscences catch the essence of the man.

Tote, while a remarkably innovative and successful crew coach, really taught sportsmanship and character. . . . Above all, he was a gentleman. Pim Goodbody '55 tells his favorite story about Tote. *My favorite story about Tote (Mr. Walker to his face and "God" behind his back) involved a race my junior year against a Princeton lightweight crew on Parents' Weekend. In those days, Kent raced against the Yale and Princeton lightweights as part of our regular schedule. Princeton had decided not to bring its own boats, so Tote went out in the launch Saturday morning (we were in class) with the Princeton coach while their teams rowed in the boats they would be racing in that afternoon. I feel sure Tote was telling the Princeton coach absolutely everything about the racecourse, such as the location of currents and dead water, so that his crews would not be at any disadvantage in the races. Anyway, the Princeton coach apparently launched into a lecture about the rowing technique that Tote taught, saying it wasn't "correct" and that any graduates of Kent crews who went to Princeton were made to change sides so they could be taught to row "right."*

In the boathouse, just before we went out for our race that afternoon, Tote told us this story. I can remember being absolutely shocked that anyone would talk to Tote that way. Tote would not let his crews win by more than two lengths. He felt winning was enough and that there was no need to humiliate the other crew. During a race, if it looked as if we were pulling away by more than two lengths, you would hear Tote call "get in your lane Kent," which was his command for us to ease off. This day Tote said, "If you want to win by more than two lengths, go ahead."

Well, I can tell you there was no more motivated crew in the world that day, and we went out and won by seven lengths using Tote's "wrong" technique, and in front of our parents no less. "Well rowed, Princeton. Well rowed, Kent" Tote called out with his megaphone after we had gotten our breaths back. What an experience!

Tote's successor was W. Hart Perry. Mr. Perry wore many hats in his years at Kent, but the one he probably loved most was that of KSBC coach. Hart Perry rowed at Noble and Greenough and Dartmouth, where he also coached. After coaching from 1956-1958 at Iolanni School in Hawaii, he came to Kent in 1961 and for the next 34 years he led Kent crews to victories at NEIRA and Henley numerous times. In 1974 he became the first non-British Commonwealth citizen elected Steward and Timekeeper at the Henley Royal Regatta, a position he continues to hold. Mr. Perry's honors are too numerous to mention here, but a

Hart Perry.

Coach Houston with three members of the KSBC.

"messing about in boats" translated to boat speed and to the confidence his teams had in knowing they had the best coach in the league. When I started coaching, a colleague told me, "If you base how you feel about yourself at the end of each day on the performance of a bunch of high school kids, you're setting yourself up for disaster." In other words, don't invest your time and energy in boys that don't have their heads screwed on right.

Maybe that's the greatest secret the godfather was able to keep all these years. Through his inordinate capacity to care about all who rowed for him, Hart Perry set himself up for disaster but knocked down the competition. Kent is proud.

tribute from one of his former students, Daniel Perkins '93, currently coaching freshman heavyweight crew at Columbia, sums up his influence.

At the dedication of a rowing shell in Hart Perry's name, Olympic gold medal-winning coach Mike Teti said, "US rowing has an executive director, a board, coaches, members; all are critical to the sport, but Hart is the godfather of US rowing. Coaches and others might come and go, but the godfather always takes care of his children."

There is so much I can't tell you about the KSBC and about rowing for Hart Perry, simply because he was and is the godfather. What I will tell you is that one sensed that he knew more about what was happening at Kent at any given moment than anyone, and he was regarded by most with a certain wary reverence. The few that didn't implicitly believe Mr. Perry was somewhere in the background pulling the strings, wanted to.

Mr. Perry watched us as students and he watched us as athletes. He watched us for potential, and probably lost sleep over making us stronger and faster oarsmen. No matter how dense boys at that age can be, they will always recognize and seek out those who are able to usher them towards manhood and, often more importantly, out of adolescence.

Yes, many coaches possess this trait, but we always knew with Mr. P. that every detail was taken care of; nothing that was his would be left to chance. The eradication of chance in a rowing race was an idea that came down from Tote Walker, Mr. Perry's predecessor. Always it was "Row well," never "Good luck." Luck was, and is, the refuge of the unprepared. Mr. Perry added to this his own love for tinkering with the rigging and the use of the latest gadgets, the best equipment, all to gain an edge on the competition. What he called

Kent's current coach, Eric Houston '80, another of Hart Perry's oarsmen, is carrying on the tradition of Kent's winning crews.

Eric Houston is everything one would expect from a KSBC coach. He was a 4-year Varsity oarsman at Kent, rowing under Coach Perry, and he captained the 1980 National Championship Crew that won the Stotesbury Cup Regatta in Philadelphia. After graduating from Trinity College, he returned to Kent to teach science and to assist Hart Perry. When Perry retired, he became head coach and has since directed the program with great success. His 1999 Henley Crew won a silver medal at the NEIRA Championships, and his 2001 Henley Crew was his first to win the NEIRA championship. In a sport that is getting more competitive every year, Coach Houston has remained a constant for every member of the KSBC in the past two decades. His knowledge of the sport is a perfect blend of intensity and technique, and his rapport with his rowers is an ideal medium of sternness and compassion. In the everchanging sport of rowing, Houston has led the boys to success into the 21st century while maintaining the ideals and traditions that KSBC was founded on in 1922 (Andrew Schneider '00, English teacher and KSBC coach).

The girls have been equally fortunate, especially in having Mark McWhinney '75 as their coach when they began racing in the spring crew season. Mr. McWhinney assisted Hart Perry when the crew program began on the Hill, and when he returned to Kent after graduating from UNC, he joined the math department. In 1981 Hart Perry made him head coach. In the years that Mr. McWhinney was coach, girls crew became one of Kent's strongest competitors, the First Eight winning

The 2002 Girls Crew triumphed at Henley.

New Englands in 1983, 1985, 1986, 1987, 1996, and 1997 and the Second Eight winning NEIRA in 1985, 1986, 1987 (second Eight). The 1986 and 1987 crews were National championship crews.

In 2006, Kent was blessed with strong boys and girls crews as all six boats entered in the New England championships in Worcester medaled. The regatta, which celebrated its 60th anniversary this year, was started by Father Sill and a few other headmasters and crew coaches. This year there were fifty-two races and 1,331 competitors. Kent's first boys boat was particularly proud that they were bringing the championship trophy, given in honor of Father Sill fifty years ago, to Kent in the School's centennial year. KSBC went on to row at Henley once again and was the first American crew to challenge for the new Prince Albert Cup. Kent won the first race, but lost to a strong Durham University in the second round.

The legacy of Father Sill, Tote Walker, Hart Perry, Mark Mc Whinney, Eric Houston, and all the other men and women who have coached Kent crew as well as the boys and girls who have rowed to victory continues into the twenty-first century.

THE KENT ORGAN

In St. Joseph's Chapel, after many years and many organs, a wonderful instrument was built. Organist Thomas Holcombe's account of the evolution of Kent's organs is a fascinating story.

SINCE THE EARLY DAYS OF THE SCHOOL, FATHER SILL as headmaster and priest had his boys singing hymns in daily chapel: as an Episcopalian brought up in the church by his father, also a priest, he inherited a strong liturgical tradition of congregational hymnody, and as an Anglo-Catholic monk of the Order of the Holy Cross he inherited an active tradition of Gregorian-chant psalmody as well. We all know how deeply committed to his Christian faith and practice of daily worship Father Sill was, but not many know that in addition to all the other things he obviously was, he was also a musician. He played the violin, and his contemporaries in the 1920s were astonished and delighted to see him come forward and play in the School dance orchestra—he was good enough to lead the violin section for a time. He obviously knew how to read music; whether he was able to get along on the piano or parlor organ well enough to accompany his students singing hymns as well, we don't know, but it seems likely. In any case, since he was trying to teach young boys to be self-reliant, to take charge and be responsible young men, and since as the celebrant he had his hands full already with non-musical concerns, he certainly wanted underlings to step forward and do the honors.

There is only one individual we know of for sure who played for the School during those early years, and that is Paul Squibb of the class of 1914—although it is hard to imagine that before him Roger Sessions of the class of 1911 did not play, as he was an able pianist who not long after this played all three movements of a Beethoven piano sonata in front of the assembled School—and of course, he went on to become a composer and the School's most famous musical alumnus.

Paul Squibb was the first student organist to play in the "new" St. Joseph's Chapel, the original wooden one, after it was finished in December 1913. When they moved the old harmonium or reed organ in, having carried it from the room adjoining the study hall where they had previously been using it, they found out right away that it really was too small for the new space. They had to make do; Father Sill, always the educator, probably excused its inadequacy by arguing that a little adversity is good for people—it brings out the spunk in those who have to grapple with it. As St. Paul wrote, "suffering produces endurance, endurance produces character." The School's reed organ lasted in gradually deteriorating condition for another five years or so: one can imagine what the original School Hymn—"O Saviour, precious Saviour" [#349 in the old 1940 Hymnal]—sounded like when played on it, with the young organist pumping as hard as he could and the chords pulsating with the wobbly vibrato produced by an unstable wind system. These instruments were really designed to accompany hymns sung in private family devotions in Victorian parlors, not to support a student congregation singing in a full chapel service!

What finally precipitated a major change was the arrival in January 1918 of George Hodges Bartlett, who had just completed a Harvard education in 3 ½ years. The older brother of two current students at the School, Bartlett showed himself right away to be an exceptional person, one of those rare individuals who could do almost anything; not only would he teach English, German and history, and according to one source, Latin and French as well, but also, being a fair pianist, he could get by on the organ, too, so he would play for daily Chapel services. He was not of strong physical constitution, but for a while that didn't seem to matter, as he clearly had a lot of energy. He was also blessed with a kindly disposition and an infectious enthusiasm which inspired those around him, including, apparently, the headmaster: within months he had gotten Father Sill to investigate how to get a pipe organ for the Chapel and contact the nearest organ builder capable of doing the work, Harry Hall of West Haven. A suitable instrument would cost the School two thousand dollars.

What Father Sill did next was typical of him: with characteristic directness and steadfastness-of-purpose he established an organ fund, publicized it in the *Kent School News*, urged students and friends to donate to it, and had the *News* inform the School community weekly as to who, starting with George Bartlett himself, had given to the fund, how much they had given, what the total in the fund was—to the penny—and how much more was needed. This is how we know to this day that already by April 6 of that year, the fund was up to $379.13, and by the 25th of October it was up to $873.23. On December 6th readers were told that Father Sill had added the Thanksgiving collection to the fund, and that had brought it up to $1250. There was a good reason why the collection on that holiday was so large: the students were not allowed to go home in those days, so they were all present, as well as many parents who had come to visit. Even so, less than two-

thirds of the needed funds had been raised—and yet Father Sill, always a man of extraordinary faith, signed the contract with the organ-builders anyway. By January 24th the fund was up to $1520, the organ men were due to arrive in another week, and posterity is left to wonder where the remaining $480 came from. It most assuredly did come, though; Father Sill seems to have had a way with money!

In any case, two men from the Hall Organ Company came on the first of February 1919, as contracted, and over the next few days installed their instrument upstairs in the back gallery of the Chapel. According to the bronze plaque affixed to the east wall of the present St. Joseph's Chapel near the stairs, George Bartlett was the first to play this organ, and served faithfully until his heart gave out and he died at home in May 1921. According to notices and articles in the *Kent School News* at the time, the community loved him and was deeply devastated by this incalculable loss.

One of the things the untimely death of George Bartlett meant was that students had to step forward again and assume responsibility for accompanying the congregational singing in Chapel. It is amazing that there were individuals who were capable of doing this, and one can't help wonder how well they played.

As far as the 1919 instrument itself is concerned, little information survives. There is one tantalizing picture, however, which shows the two keyboards and pedals built right into the center front of the paneled case, with a side-to-side display of open diapason pipes standing on the impost molding just above the music rack, in three wide flats. One can deduce something about this organ if one assumes that it was basically similar to organs the Hall Organ Company installed elsewhere, a few of which are remembered by old-timers in the organ maintenance business in this region. Posterity has not been kind to their legacy: most of their instruments have long since been replaced. One can deduce a lot about the Kent organ if one assumes that it was basically the same as the instrument the Hall people later installed in the new stone St. Joseph's in 1931—which based on the evidence is highly likely. After all, the organ was only a dozen years old at that time. The instrument as it was in

1931 survived until 1956, so there are people still living today who remember it from their youth, and they can give a pretty good idea of what it was like.

This much is clear: in accordance with the taste of the time the original St. Joseph's organ was not designed to play any of the great organ repertoire properly, as any experienced organist today would insist that it be able to do, but rather just to accompany hymns and sacred solos of a type that are no longer heard nowadays, being considered dated and mediocre in quality. What preludes and postludes the student organists played on this organ is not clear, but it is probably safe to assume that they played selections from a few tattered old collections of topical period pieces, over and over, as best as they were able. The instrument can only have produced the sort of tubby, muddy ensemble sound which a modern professional organist would consider very unattractive.

Who were these student organists? One may glean the following from the yearbooks of that era: Frederick Portmas Wegner 1922, William Brewster 1923-24, Garrett Coerte Voorhees 1925-26, Robert John Kinney 1927, Charles Price Britton 1928, Herbert William Smith 1929, George Warren Hayes 1930, Peter Kimball Page 1931-32.

As suggested, one assumes that in 1931 the Hall Organ Co. people removed this organ from the gallery of the old St. Joseph's, took it to their shop in West Haven, worked it over, provided a new "Organ-Supply" type console for it, and brought it back. The new console was necessary because in the new Chapel the organ's main case, containing the swell-box, wind-chests, pipes and reservoir, would be in a special loft or balcony upstairs above the north aisle, while the console accommodating the player would be located elsewhere, downstairs on the north side of the chancel, around the corner of the chancel arch. The blower would be in the basement, with its wind-duct passing up inside the wall for two stories, opening into the balcony, and connecting to the reservoir there standing on the floor of the loft with the rest of the organ immediately above it. In fact, in the chapel basement to this day one can see the lower end of this duct, which still has the old canvas skirt on it that connected the duct to the blower itself,

until the instrument was discarded in 1956.

From a discriminating organist's perspective this installation must have been very unsatisfactory since for the player the heavy masonry of the chancel arch was in the way, blocking the direct passage of sound from the pipes; he of all people must have been the one least able to hear what he was playing! No reputable organ-builder today would arrange an installation like this, with the pipes so remote from the organist.

The students who played this organ proudly claimed the title of "School organist" in their respective yearbooks, so we know who they were:

John Holbrook Park, 1942–44
John Robert Miller, 1944–47
Horace Gray Lunt II, 1935–37
John Knott Maxwell, 1947–50
Richard Morehouse Booth, 1937–38
Alan Osborn Dann, 1948–51
Edward Bradford Walker, 1940–41
Stephen Squires Garmey, 1950–52
Douglas Graham Smythe, 1941
David Price Jenkins, 1951-54
Robert Charles Derr, 1941–43
Donald Leonard Robinson, 1952–54
David Page Harris, 1942–44
John Leverett Davenport, 1954
Charles Gomph Newbery, 1943–46
George Henry Wehmeyer, 1951–55

By the 1950s the Kent organ was suffering from a variety of mechanical problems, and it would soon need a major rebuilding. This would be expensive, and when it was completed the School would still have the mediocre instrument it started with. The alternative, even more expensive, was to replace the organ altogether. This was the time of the so-called "Organ reform," and taste in both what sort of musical literature one wanted to play and what sort of instrument was going to be suitable for it had changed dramatically. An up-to-date church musician in 1955 would have strongly preferred to start over with a completely new instrument, and such was Father William Penfield: Father Penfield had just come to the School as a young man in 1955, and being an organist as well as a priest, he would be the one responsible for the Chapel music from then on.

Ever since the German philosopher Hegel identified the phenomenon a couple of centuries ago, historians of cultural evolution have noticed the way people's tastes change with the passing of time, how people often come to reject what came immediately before them and go to the opposite extreme—which Hegel called the "antithesis." So it was back in the '50s and '60s in the organ business: there was a very different spirit in the air, and in the interests of raising the standards of the music they performed, professionals rejected the mediocre, dated repertoire of their immediate past, and the tubby-sounding organs designed to play it. Instead they wanted to play the newly-rediscovered organ literature of the Baroque era, and demanded organs whose thin and bright, even 'screechy' ensemble sound seemed appropriate for this music.

So it was that in 1956 the Kent School authorities, doubtless considering themselves very up-to-date, entered into a contract with Walter Holtkamp of the Cleveland-based Holtkamp Organ Company for them to provide a radically new instrument for St. Joseph's Chapel. In the first place, its pipes had to be out in the open where they could be readily heard, and the organist had to be in close proximity so he could hear best of all. Furthermore, there had to be adequate seating space nearby to accommodate the Choir, who years before had been bumped out of their original place in the chancel stalls. The only place in the building where all these needs could be met was at the west end, so that was where the team from Cleveland placed the new organ, hanging it on the back wall under and partly in front of Len Howard's beautiful rose window. This took place during the week following their arrival on the 28th of May, 1956.

As for their choice of organ-builder, one should realize that this was the time when the Holtkamp firm was at the 'cutting edge' of the great reform, and they were installing new instruments in a number of prominent places. One need only mention the Chapel at General Theological Seminary in New York, Saarinen's

stunning Chapel at M.I.T (where a Holtkamp organ almost identical to the 1956 Kent instrument hangs on the wall to this day), also the modern Auditorium at M.I.T., and even more impressively, the Battell Chapel at Yale, where a large instrument in the north transept incorporates a small chancel division which is also much like the Kent organ.

In trade journals for organists the Holtkamp people used to advertise the "limitations" of their organs, as if limitations in an organ were a virtue, and the 1956 organ at Kent had plenty of them: without much bass, and no 8' principal, it supported congregational singing poorly. Without a swell division it didn't accompany a choir very well either. It also lacked 'reed' and 'string' stops, so a lot of the more recent organ literature couldn't be registered properly. It did have a clean and bright sound, however, and seemed to be pretty well-made. Word has it that people were disappointed with the new Kent organ after it was installed, but for the money the School could afford to pay for it, the Holtkamp people couldn't have been fairly expected to do much more. In any case, the little 1956 organ served reliably for over 30 years, and successive adult organists John Hinners, Franklin Coleman, and Tom Holcombe played a great deal of fine music on it, including much from the Romantic and modern eras, most of which was never going to sound right on it because the instrument lacked the appropriate tonal resources. The practice of student organists continued for a while after 1956, but gradually petered out; part of the reason for this may have been the clear and bright voicing of the new organ, which inevitably made student wrong notes painfully obvious to the listener. The following should be named: Clifford Chapin Conway 1953-57; Louis Parker Buck III 1959; Aims Chamberlain McGuinness1954-58; Stuart Hay Chamberlain, Jr. 1961. As far as the adult organists of that era were concerned, Father Penfield stayed at Kent until 1964, John Hinners served as organist from 1965 to 1971, Franklin Coleman from 1971 to 1976, George Dampe briefly during the fall of 1976, and the present incumbent (and writer) from the fall of 1977 to the present time.

I beg the reader's forbearance if I continue this

history in the first person, because it really is my story as much as anyone else's. The long and convoluted process of getting the new large organ in St. Joseph's began sometime back in the early '80s, when I wistfully observed to my old friend from college days, the organ-builder Jeremy Cooper, that the Holtkamp organ was woefully inadequate, and wouldn't it be nice to get a substantial instrument in the lovely Kent School Chapel, so I could perform a wide variety of great organ music there and actually have it sound right. What could be more appropriate, considering that the students had frequent required services to attend, and I felt I had an educational responsibility to expose them to great church-music? Besides, the Episcopal Church has long had a tradition of distinguished music which is well worth perpetuating. As far as a new large organ was concerned, it would be nice to combine something of the fullness and bass of the 1919/1931 organ with the brilliance and clarity of the 1956 Holtkamp, and arrive at a Hegelian "synthesis," an instrument which would be much more flexible and accommodating for a wide variety of musical demands.

Not so long after that Mr. Cooper learned of an old organ, approximately the same size as the 1919 and 1956 Kent organs combined, which was available for re-location: it stood in the front of the Universalist Church in his hometown, Concord, New Hampshire, and it had to be removed soon, as the church was slated to be torn down. This instrument had been built in Boston back in 1907, by the firm which since their beginning in the 1830s has generally in the business been considered to be the greatest American organ-builder of the time, Hook and Hastings; and despite its age the instrument appeared to still be in pretty good condition. This organ could easily be substantially enlarged by the addition of a third manual—the Choir—the wind-chest and pipes of which could be placed in a void in the back of the interior of the case seemingly left by the original builders for this very purpose. Also, it had most of the large and therefore most expensive pipes already, so adding a variety of higher-pitched stops to give it greater brilliance could be done at relatively low cost. Jeremy Cooper, undaunted by the fact that he had never done such a large instrument before, seemed anxious to do the work.

It was hard for Headmaster Father Schell to give his approval for this project, partly because it was so unclear what would be involved or how much it would cost, and there was so little political support around the institution for such a risky venture. However, he dared to take a big chance, bade me pursue the project with Mr. Cooper, and helped arrange for the consortium of lawyers now in charge of the Concord property to donate the instrument to the School as a tax write-off.

So it came to pass that during several freezing-cold days after Christmas 1985 a crew of five or so workers including myself gathered at the Concord church with empty boxes and crates, tubs for all sizes of screws, an assortment of screwdrivers and other tools, and a portable space-heater which we presently got roaring away in the vain attempt to raise the temperature in the abandoned church to at least the freezing point. In this enterprise we were led by the late Alan Laufman, founder and long-time director of the "Organ Clearing House," and organ-builder Jeremy Cooper was there, too. It took us several days to dismantle the instrument and spread its pieces all over the interior of the church, then finally load them into a large truck for conveyance to Mr. Cooper's shop, where they were brought in and stored for several years while he figured out what he was going to do to rebuild the instrument.

In June 1990 people from the Peebles-Herzog firm of Columbus, Ohio, arrived at Kent, dismantled the Holtkamp organ, and transported it to their shop, where they enlarged it slightly, made good on some of its worst limitations, and eventually installed it in a Roman Catholic church in Ohio.

That cleared the way for Jeremy Cooper and me to drive van loads of large and heavy organ parts from his shop outside Concord, New Hampshire, down to Kent, and soon the back of the Chapel was filled with reconditioned chests, pipe-trays, oaken case-front panels, planks and boards. By September Cooper and his wife had enough of the organ together for some of it to be playable. They continued all fall and through the winter, only gradually realizing that there were some serious

Organist and choirmaster Thomas Holcombe at the console of the organ.

design problems for which their careful craftsmanship was not going to be enough to compensate. By the late spring the organ was 80-to-90% finished, and with some difficulty playable: it sounded good, and looked good, too, even though it was not yet complete. However, there was a serious manual key-action problem: the touch was much too heavy to be acceptable. Also, the wind ducts to the new pedal chests seemed too small to convey enough air when all the new stops were in. What's more, the pedal action involved long rollers that 'torqued' so badly that they were unable to pull the big pedal pallets open far enough. At this point the organ-builder, exhausted and frustrated, ran out of funds and had to leave, leaving me with a playable but unfinished instrument, and the Headmaster in a politically awkward situation with the board of trustees as well.

The subsequent months turned into years, and various experts were summoned to inspect the instrument and advise the School as to the best way to proceed with the project. Eventually Alan Laufman came and advised the School to contract with Roy Redman of Fort Worth, Texas, to come and complete the job—and so it was that Mr. Redman and his team of men and women came, in the summer of '96, dismantled the organ once again, loaded it into an enormous trailer truck, and packed it off to Texas. There followed lengthy telephone discussions as to what the Redman people were going to do with

it, and we decided that besides replacing the key action and the wind system they should enlarge the instrument further, to make it even more complete. Only gradually did it become apparent to me that they were completely re-engineering the instrument from the floor up, and it would have two complete key actions: the desired mechanical action virtually throughout, but also an assisting electric pull-down action to lighten the touch and make the organ easily playable. The wind system would all be new, too. There would also be a new reversed-and-detached console out front . . . and many other things would be changed as well.

Roy Redman and his crew brought the transformed instrument back in midsummer '97, and I had the pleasure of helping them to erect it as it now stands. Some of this was hard physical work: lifting the heavy wind-chests up into their several positions inside the case, also the large wooden double-open-diapason pipes up to their positions in back, and the big metal "sub-bass" pipes in the front "pedal-towers." Luckily, this time things went without a hitch, and the finished organ played beautifully. As completed, the organ has a replacement value of something on the order of $800,000, and we paid less than half of that; it's hard to see how Roy Redman and his crew could have made any money on the project, but they clearly took satisfaction from having created something great. The instrument is now three times its original size, and far better than ever before. One doesn't have to understand all the technical jargon to see that the new St. Joseph's Chapel organ has extensive resources and can give a good account of almost any literature, from any period, that one might choose to play on it. Of all the other great New England prep schools, only St. Paul's and Groton have instruments that are comparable in size and quality.

—Thomas Holcombe, Organist and Choirmaster

V
A NOBLER SCHOOL

IN THE TWENTY-FIVE YEARS SINCE HIS INSTITUTION IN ST. JOSEPH'S CHAPEL as headmaster and rector, Richardson Whitfield Schell has helped Kent to become one of the foremost schools in New England, indeed in the country. From the beginning, Father Schell was involved in all areas of School life, continuing to teach in the first years of his headmastership. However, it was clear to him that one of his top priorities was to make Kent financially stable. This took him three years, and it led to the realization that in order to survive long term the School would have to streamline its operations.

In February 1984, the trustees and headmaster began a process of deliberation which culminated in the consolidation of the two campuses eight years later. At the time, various projects were under consideration, including the renovation of the Dining Hall dorm in the Valley and a proposed arts center on the Hill. At the May 1984 meeting of the board, the trustees passed a resolution stating that the School should engage the services of the Carlson Group to "execute a preliminary master plan" for the School, and further resolved "that Kent School undertake an internal ten-year long-range planning study and that a preliminary report be available for the Trustees at their fall meeting" (Summary of the Proceedings on Consolidation of The Board of Trustees 1984-1990). This resolution was followed by further meetings discussing the launching of a capital campaign to be announced publicly no sooner than 1986.

By May 1985, the trustees were discussing the consolidation of the Hill and Valley campuses, and three committees were appointed. The Concept Committee, chaired by Robert A. Ward '53, vice-president of the board, was to study the educational and social considerations of consolidation; its members were O.B. Davis '42, chairman, English department; Laurance B. Rand III, chairman, history department; Loretto S. Roney, director of studies; Donald K. Gowan '66, dean of boys; Peter H. Conze '38, president, board of trustees; Judith B. Wentz, trustee; Cornelia K. Biddle '64, trustee; Richardson W. Schell '69, headmaster; Claude Saucy, chairman, art department; Lizanne S. Mulligan '75, assistant dean of girls; Louisa M. LaFontan, dean of girls; Charles B. Colmore, Jr. '31, trustee; William D. Hawkins '30, trustee; and John S. Kerr, director of girls admissions.

The Real Estate Committee, chaired by George Vila, was to study

Above: Father Schell joined the Kent faculty as chairman of the theology department and chaplain in 1980.

Below: Robert A. Ward '53.

the question of land availability at the Boys School; and the Budget Committee, chaired by Ann Dickinson '65, was to study the economics of a consolidated school. Lawrence Lieberfeld of Peat, Marwick & Mitchell was engaged to conduct a study of the feasibility of the merger of the two campuses.

Robert A. Ward '53 had prepared a statement that the trustees then used to respond to inquiries from the press and the alumni body.

To remain healthy every institution must from time to time reexamine the presuppositions on which its existence is based. A quarter of a century ago Kent School boldly moved to make its educational opportunities available to young women. It chose to do so in a coordinate mode by building a second campus for girls. Twenty-five years later the Board of Trustees, in considering the oncoming need to refurbish that campus and to provide additional, much needed facilities there, has prudently decided to ask again the fundamental question relating to the mode chosen in 1959. Simply put that question is: Will we continue to subscribe to the coordinate mode or will we seek some new arrangement—to make both campuses coeducational or to consolidate on one fully coeducational campus?

The Board, facing the investment of multiple millions of dollars in whatever may be the answer to that question, has established three special committees to review the relevant factors. Two of those committees—one on Plant and a second on Operating Finances—will deal with the tangibles that can be quantified. The third—a so-called Concept Committee to look at the philosophical implications of maintaining the status quo or making some change—will deal with the intangibles, the educational and institutional pluses and minuses involved.

The three committees will work closely together. If the Concept Committee finds that the pluses outweigh the minuses for a move to consolidation—and the other two groups find such a move to be feasible and practical, the Board will face that decision and the resulting need to raise and deploy the monies necessary to accomplish such a change. If that change appears infeasible and the costs prohibitive, the Board will seek to raise and deploy the requisite funds to enhance its coordinate mode, realizing that the pluses for consolidation are conversely the minuses for the current configuration—and move to reduce and, as far as possible, eliminate those negatives by whatever arrangements are necessary.

Whatever the outcome of this review, Kent School will enter its ninth decade in 1986, positioned to face the future with its traditional values intact and its structure strengthened. Before we move into that future, however, it is appropriate—indeed mandatory—that we take a hard look at the "ifs" before us. We are at an important moment in our institutional evolution, and we will not permit that moment to pass without careful examination. In a sense, this review will afford Kent School a timely opportunity to check the stars it steers by — and better chart the course ahead. (May 27, 1985)

At the trustees meeting on April 18, 1986, Peter Conze '38 summarized Kent's position in connection with the consolidation project and, after a full discussion and motions made and seconded, it was unanimously "RESOLVED: That (1) the Board of Trustees accept and unanimously endorses the Concept Committee's specific recommendation of June 24, 1985, that Kent School

ROBERT A. WARD '53

Bob Ward grew up in Kent. His father was a maintenance worker at the School, and when it was time for Bob to go to high school, he received a scholarship to Kent. His qualities of leadership were immediately apparent, and he served as Senior Prefect of the Class of 1953. When he graduated, he went on to Amherst College, where he later served as Dean of Students. He taught English at Loomis-Chafee, where the Ward Bowl, awarded to either Kent or Loomis—whichever school wins all the games except football (for which the Spoon is awarded) on Loomis Day—was given in his honor. At Amherst, the Ward Room was named for Bob. His last academic post was as headmaster of Williston Academy. He retired in 1979 at forty-five to take care of his aging parents in Kent. But that was not the end of his service. Bob was elected First Selectman of the town of Kent, perhaps one of the best the town has had. At Kent, he was vice president of the board of trustees and a member of the headmaster search committee which chose Richardson W. Schell to be Kent's sixth headmaster. After he returned to the town of Kent, he continued to teach as a visiting faculty member in English. Bob's specialty was Robert Frost, and Marel Rogers '65, Kent's librarian, recalls that she first met Bob "after he had retired from being First Selectman and was teaching a seminar on Robert Frost on the Valley campus in 1984 or 1985. He would stop in the library office to use the photocopier, and be assailed by the library director, Bill John, who shared Bob's interest in Frost. Bill expressed his interest by reciting Frost's works to Bob. Always polite, Bob never interrupted—even when the poem was 'The Death of the Hired Man.'" O.B. Davis remembers the memorable day when General Douglas MacArthur came to Kent. "Bob Ward, along with his very impressive list of serious accomplishments, was richly endowed with the comic sense, and with the wit and boldness to enjoy putting that sense into action. That is, Bob was an accomplished trickster." O.B.'s tale of Bob's best opportunity for trickery is memorable, for Bob arrived on campus, in full uniform, corn cob pipe clenched in his teeth, sunglasses, standing in the back of O.B.'s Ford convertible, the spitting image of MacArthur. And it took a few minutes before someone, a second former O.B. recalls, "squeaked clearly, 'Hey, that's Bob Ward.'" Bob will be remembered at Kent for his many gifts, and it is fitting that this man whose life was so much a part of the School should be remembered by having a road in the Skiff Mountain faculty housing complex named for him.

consolidate on the Valley Campus; [and] that (2) it become a school of 525 boarding students and up to 25 day students . . . ."

On June 1, 1986, the *Kent News* reported that Peter H. Conze '38, president of the Board of Trustees, had announced that after a year of internal study that included students, faculty, trustees, and consultants, the Board had unanimously endorsed recommendations by the special Faculty and Trustee Concept Committee that Kent School consolidate on one campus. Sadly, Robert A. Ward, who had given so much of himself to this committee, died only six months later, on November 20, 1986, and never saw the work of his committee come to fruition.

The financing of such a major building program was certainly one of the major challenges facing the board of trustees. Based on the estimate of the Sordini Construction Company, the total construction cost would be almost $23,000,000. Some of this would come from the capital campaign then underway, some from the sale of the hill campus, and a substantial portion

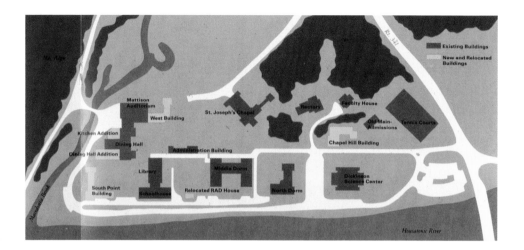

from borrowing. Fortunately the Connecticut Health and Education Facilities Authority (CHEFA) had recently enacted legislation which made it possible for the School to finance the entire cost of the project on a tax-exempt basis on favorable terms. Kent was one of the first schools to take advantage of this new legislation.

Next came the task of selecting architects to design the buildings that would be needed: a new classroom building, two new dormitories, and an addition to the Dining Hall. The Architect Selection Committee, chaired by Arthur Collins '48, chose Stecker, LaBau, Arneill, McManus Architects, Inc. of Hartford to create a Campus Master Plan and they finally were chosen to plan and supervise the construction of the consolidated campus. S/L/A/M's Campus Master Plan is well worth quoting as a reminder of the challenges faced by the architects, especially the fact that while the School owns "land in abundance . . . much of that land is either so low in elevation as to be flood-prone or so mountainous as to be, for all practical purposes, inaccessible."

Below: The Dining Hall.

Another challenge was to place new construction on the ridge above the flood plain without compromising the sense of space that existed on the campus as it was in 1987 when the plan was conceived. The central green is "a place that has been shaped over time and, in this process, it has acquired a great meaning of its own. Facing onto this green are many of the most important institutions of the Kent community: Chapel, Administration, Dining, Meeting, Housing, Classrooms, and Library. It is for these reasons that it is appropriate to compare this space to

a New England Village Green. Such places are rarely geometrically formal and yet always charged with meaning. . . . [It] is rarely a closed square. It is instead permeable. People can come and go from many different directions. A closed square sets itself apart from its surrounding. A village green opens itself up as if to include the rest of the community.

"At Kent the central green is visually and physically open in many directions. In doing so the green is tied to all the other spaces of the campus, not only to the other courts between buildings which surround the green, but also to the natural setting beyond. There are views of the Housatonic River, the mountains across the river, Mount Algo, Chapel Hill, Fuller Mountain and to the west, Macedonia Valley. Each of the other man-made spaces on the campus maintains a similar visible permeability, none is an enclosed courtyard. In this way spaces which are relatively small seem far larger. At the same time the enormity of the natural site features is filtered through a man-made screen that returns the space to a human proportion. It is this interplay between the natural and man-made elements which gives Kent its special character."

Ground-breaking took place after Prize Day in June 1990, and two years later, in September 1992, Kent School again opened on one campus.

Those who were at Kent during the two years between the groundbreaking for the first new building to be constructed and the first day of classes on the consolidated campus in September 1992 saw buildings disappear, move,

Above: (Top) As part of the consolidation of the two campuses, the RAD House was moved to its present location facing the Administration Building. (Bottom) The RAD House.
Right: Case Dorm from the Dining Hall.

and spring up, sometimes apparently as they watched. The old infirmary, the first brick, fire-proof building on Father Sill's campus, was razed to make way for a new dorm. The RAD House was moved to its current location, creating an open courtyard with Middle Dorm to the north, Schoolhouse to the south, and the Administration Building to the west. Its progress from its old location, as it moved inch by inch past Schoolhouse, was watched with fascination by everyone who had a spare minute. Case Dorm was built on the south point of the campus at the confluence of Macedonia Brook and the Housatonic, affording its residents one of the best river views in Connecticut.

The new Health Center, dedicated in honor of Tracy Dickinson '73, moved into the lowest floor of Case. The library, expanded to fill one full floor of Schoolhouse, and the music complex were both renovated. Girls' locker rooms and enlarged training facilities were added to Magowan Field House, and new athletic fields, south of the campus on Schaghticoke Road, were ready for the girls field hockey and boys soccer teams. The Dining Hall was expanded, and the area at the south end was dedicated to Tote Walker. On the lower level of that extension were the Stat Store and the student center with a snack bar and student mailboxes. Field Dormitory was a northward extension of Mattison, affording the art department new classrooms and studios on its lowest floor, all overlooking the Macedonia Valley. A new classroom building to house the English and history departments, dedicated in memory of Gifford T. Foley '65, sprang up across the walk from the science building. One young man, coming out of Dickinson after a class, said he was astonished to find the steel skeleton of a building where he remembered seeing nothing when he went into that

HADLEY CASE '29

Hadley Case is one of Kent's great alumni, a man who gave much to the School he loved, serving as chairman of the 50th anniversary committee and member of the Vance Committee that opened Kent to girls in 1960, as trustee, as corporation treasurer, and as chancellor. When he graduated from Kent, he thanked Father Sill: "I want to thank you, Pater, for all that you have done for me at Kent . . . I always will uphold my old school, for I certainly am proud of it." And uphold it he did, giving his time, talent, energy, and treasure to the School, and becoming one its greatest benefactors.

A graduate of Antioch College, Hadley Case joined a mining company based in London and was assigned to Australia, where he made aerial photographic maps. He later joined Case, Pomeroy & Company in New York City, and was elected president of the company in 1941. He established a worldwide reputation in the oil, gas, and minerals industry.

When Case Dormitory was dedicated on May 15, 1992, Peter Conze '38, then chairman of the board of

Hadley Case '29.

trustees, paid tribute to Hadley Case, saying, "I can say without exaggeration that the post-war history of Kent School is intertwined—for the good—with the life and career of Hadley Case. There is hardly a structure at the School that does not owe its existence, to a greater or lesser degree, to the generosity of Hadley Case: the boat house, the hockey rink, the field house, the dormitory on the Hill. Hadley has been generous to an extreme."

On the occasion of his death, the board of trustees passed a Resolution of Thanks for the Life of Hadley Case:

"Whereas he was instrumental as a member of the Vance Committee in helping to extend Kent's vision to encompass opportunity for young women as well as young men through the creation of the Girls School;

"Whereas he gave generously of his time, talent and treasure in giving birth to Kent's Centennial Master Plan through the consolidation of campuses;

"Whereas he helped significantly in setting us on the right path toward endowment growth and on several occasions literally saved his School from certain economic pressures that threatened it;

"Whereas all he did for Kent he did with incomparable sweetness, humility, good cheer, selfless sacrifice, and an unshakable and infectious optimism, and all with the approving eye of his beloved wife, Betty;

"Be it therefore resolved that the Board of Trustees hereby gives thanks for the life and good works of Hadley Case. If ever there was a heart that awoke 'in young content' between these 'hills and river shore,' surely one of the greatest was Hadley's. He remembered so well his 'dawn at Kent.' The dawn of this School's second century will be the brighter for the quality of his remembrance. May we all take inspiration from him, and may it be brighter for the quality of our own as well."

Above: (Top) The John Gray Park '28 Library today. (Bottom) Foley Hall.
Right: Field Dormitory.

class earlier in the day. During the two years it took to complete, Kent's building project was the largest one in Connecticut and possibly the largest, at one time, in independent school history. Furthermore, it is important to note that during that massive construction project everyone—builders, faculty, staff, students, visitors—was safe. The only injury was a broken rib. When construction was completed, out of mud and rocky holes came a consolidated Kent School, one, moreover, that looked as if it had always been there. And at its center, as it had since 1931, stood St. Joseph's Chapel.

How did the girls and, especially, the alumnae who had made the Hill their home feel? The current generation welcomed the changes; life without running to catch a Bluebird down the hill for classes—or standing hopefully waiting for a teacher going up or down to come along if one had missed the bus—was certainly simpler. Some of the traditions made the journey to the Valley with the girls. The Ring Banquet continued. Ethel appeared and disappeared on various paths on the Valley campus. It was easier to find a teacher for extra help or conversation. Perhaps Ann Dickinson '65 put it best: "The Hill was a special place, full of memories of friendships, learning, worship, and athletic contests. Kent is all about the people who make it up and the time we spent together. Moving to the Valley doesn't harm those memories—to me it feels like coming home to finally be full partners in the original Kent School."

OTIS BENSON DAVIS '42

As Kent School celebrates its 100th year, it is fitting that the Kent community also acknowledge and celebrate the life and continuing career of Otis Benson Davis '42, the School's Senior Master. After relinquishing chairmanship of Kent's English Department in 1988, O.B. has continued classroom instruction and today is Kent's longest-serving active teacher.

Many Kent teachers, coaches and administrators have had strong, positive impact upon their students, both in the classroom and on the playing fields "between the hills and river shore." Yet for countless graduates, and surely for me, O.B. Davis stands well in the foreground among those whom one could justifiably rank as peerless. He is, in truth, "beyond classification."

O.B. is a quintessential "man of Kent." In his student years, he first came to the School as a Third Former in the autumn of 1938. Thereafter he participated in Kent's choir and glee club; was active in dramatics and the Shakespeare Society of the day. He played football and baseball, wrestled, and rowed club crew.

Otis Benson Davis '42.

Upon graduation in 1942, along with many of his classmates, he went directly into the nation's armed forces, serving in the Army with the rank of Lieutenant. He saw active duty in Europe as a platoon and company commander in the 44th Infantry Division.

O.B. returned to Kent in 1949, joining its English Department after receiving his undergraduate degree with honors from Princeton, and completing graduate programs both at Johns Hopkins and Middlebury. Not many years later he became chair of the English Department, and served in that capacity from 1954 until retirement from the position in 1988. Since then he has been Kent School's Senior Master.

During his career he served the School in many capacities: Faculty Committee, Religious Education Committee, Discipline Committee, and Columbia Cup Committee. He was for many years head coach of varsity wrestling, successfully guiding the team to several Founder's League and New England preparatory school championships. He was also an able and enthusiastic junior varsity football coach and coach of club crews. Importantly, O.B. assisted Dr. Kenneth Clark found a series of race relations seminars at the School in the 1950s. And it should surprise no one that he directed a number of Shakespearean stage productions.

Beyond classroom English instruction, O.B. authored or co-authored a number of books and anthologies; acted as a College Board Examination reader; was president of the Town of Kent's Library Association; and sat on the town's Board of Education.

Those were, so to say, "the facts." He was and is a man of great talent, courage, accomplishment, and civic-sensibility.

But beyond the biographical peg-points there is a far more significant dimension and characteristic of his life and presence at Kent School. He was indeed an English teacher; yet he did more than merely teach the subject. For me, and I know full well for many other Kent graduates as well, O.B. Davis had the intent and skill to teach his students "how to think."

How easily comes to memory his signature classroom entrance as he intoned: "Gentlemen, seize a piece

(continued)

of paper!" And off we would go into yet another round of expository writing exercises. Faulty though my recollection may be, I know for certain that O.B.'s students did A TON of writing! Essays, short-stories, even poems—we wrote and we wrote. And we wrote! And all the while he critiqued and critiqued. And we began to learn that clear THINKING was the requisite prelude to WRITING clearly. It must have

Otis Benson Davis '42.

been from some one of O.B.'s classes that George Orwell's classic gem of a phrase comes to mind: "Modern English, especially written English, is full of bad habits which spread by imitation and which can be avoided if one is willing to take the necessary trouble. If one can get rid of these habits one can think more clearly."

Kent students over the years have read more than Orwell, written much for, and been guided by, countless fine instructors in many academic disciplines. Still, without doubt, O.B. Davis, Kent's Senior Master, must take his place among the best pedagogues and mentors that Kent School has offered over its ten decades.

He was my teacher, and later a colleague—and always a friend. So to you, Otis Benson Davis, Class of 1942, may I offer profoundest thanks for your life and career, for what you have done and still do for me and others. As the Kent community proceeds in celebration of the School's glorious centenary, I know others will join in and say: "Stay well, O.B., stay well!"

—Brandon W. Sweitzer '60

Right: Students leaving Foley with the Rectory on the hill.

Left: At the Ring Banquet, held every spring, the fifth form girls receive their Kent rings.

For the boys, too, life had changed. No longer was the Valley campus their territory alone. For some of them, this may have seemed like a loss of sorts, but they were soon aware that the gains far outweighed any losses. There were far more really co-educational classes. In the Bluebird days, not every student commuted to the other campus. The boys who had taken a first period class on the Hill certainly did not miss running for the 7:30 AM bus up the hill for a 7:50 AM first block class. Also, Roman Catholic boys no longer had to take the bus up to St. Mark's Chapel on the Hill for Mass on Sunday, for now the Roman Catholic mass was offered in town at Sacred Heart. In so many ways, life had become less hectic. It was easier for the students to know each other, to meet together in various clubs and organizations, and to establish friendships, making the environment more relaxed and, probably, healthier.

Below: Science classes, here a chemistry class with department chair Peter Goodwin, play an important role in the education of a Kent student.

In the years that followed the first burst of building, the science building was renovated so that it finally fit in architecturally with the rest of the campus. The expanded classroom space was a boon to the department, and the Studies Office and College Guidance offices moved into one of the extensions, called pods, built on the four corners of the old building. Schoolhouse was renovated, and the John Gray Park '28 Library welcomed the new space for the Archives and a third level of stacks afforded it when Schoolhouse dorm was emptied. To make up for the lost dorm

EDWARD F. DE VILLAFRANCA

Coe de Villafranca served Kent for most of his professional life, acting as chairman of the science department, director of studies, college counselor, and coordinator of the International Baccalaureate program. In Kent he served as the chairman of the Inland Wetlands Commission and was particularly effective in the area of local land use. He was also chairman of the Republican Town Committee. At his memorial service, Father Schell paid tribute to Coe. Excerpts from that eulogy follow.

"I know what the faculty mean when they say [Coe] was a teacher's teacher. . . . What I learned from Coe abut schools and science and international understanding could fill a book.

"Generations of Kent students have said and will say 'He was the best teacher I ever had.' How proud he must have been of those generations of scientifically literate young women and men whom he taught in class and instructed through the advanced placement and international baccalaureate institutes. How specially proud he must have been of the Kent students who went on to become doctors and scientists. In recent years our paths would cross at Sharon Hospital, where he was making his rounds as a volunteer. It must have occurred to him that over the years he himself had trained and inspired an entire medical staff of physicians and surgeons, nurses, lab technicians, researchers and EMTs—from the Mayo Clinic to the Kent Fire Department.

Edward F. de Villafranca.

"He was a school man. At School he made sure everything ran well. Chairman of the science department, director of studies, and college counselor and coordinator of the IB, Coe always put the interests of his students first, and he mentored and guided generations of teachers as well as students. He was nationally recognized for his work in advanced placement chemistry. A teacher's teacher.

"He was also a sportsman; a great coach of basketball, tennis, and soccer. His fellow teachers and coaches . . . have lost a pillar of Kent athletics. Still, we have gained a lasting example of fair play and good sportsmanship.

"Coe was one of the makers of the modern Kent. He arrived on the eve of the 50th year, and as a young scholar from Yale and industry he contributed to the year-long symposium on the Idea of Christian Education. Scientist, humanist, believer, Coe embodied both the ancient ideals of Benedictine learning and modern scientific knowledge to make his classroom, his laboratory, his team, his school the very best that it could be.

"Coe was a man of prayer. He knew and lived what the early church fathers taught: The key to happiness is contemplative prayer. His advice to us on more than one occasion was, 'Be sure to think it through.'

"Coe served his family, his community, the local hospital, our nation, the world of learning and, not least, his beloved church and school in Kent, with unfailing devotion and conviction. We can hear the words of our Lord himself echoed in the hymn, 'Servant, well done'" (*Kent Quarterly*, Summer 2002).

rooms, North Dorm was enlarged.

Athletics continued to fill an important niche at Kent. In 1999, the Nadal hockey rink, part of the Richard A. Springs, Jr.' 36 Center for Sports and Special Events, was enclosed, thereby becoming a multi-season facility, which could be used by various organizations year round and which would be a much more comfortable venue for fans cheering on Kent hockey. Boys and girls varsity and junior varsity teams flourished in almost every major sport, and football and crew, especially, continued to win championships. While the Hill campus had been sold to the

Above: The Chapel, Foley, North Dorm, and Dickinson.

Marvelwood School, the stables had not been sold, and the Kent Equestrian program, with space for approximately twenty-eight riders, continued to attract young riders, many of whom competed nationally. In 2002, Kent girls went to Henley for the first time and came home triumphant, having won the Peabody Cup.

With Kent now on one campus, a new home for the headmaster and a

Below: The campus in 2005.

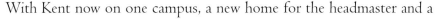

Right: Riding in the fall.

gathering place was needed. Cumming House, the new Headmaster's Residence, was built down where the farm had been. It soon became an important part of the life of the School as it is not only Father Schell's residence but also the location for a myriad of social and cultural activities. Trustees, alumni, and parent groups hold meetings and dinners there, and trustees and faculty members visit over dinner there when the Board meets. One of the highlights for some of the oldest reunion classes is having their Friday night reunion dinner at Cumming House, bringing together alumni and their spouses and the headmaster for an evening of celebration as well as a time to learn about the School today. Small groups of students with special interests meet with speakers on various subjects, and student musicians give Sunday afternoon recitals. In many years the first Seder of Passover is celebrated at Cumming House, as is the Chinese New Year. Faculty social gatherings bring together teachers from boarding schools in Litchfield County. And in September at the beginning of the academic year it is the site of a gala faculty-staff dinner.

Below: Cumming House.

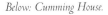

One of the loveliest additions to the campus is the Armstrong Gate, built at the main entrance to the School in 1995. Given in honor of Bill by his three children the arches contain words that epitomize Bill Armstrong's message to his third formers, a passage from Hesiod's *Work and Days*: "Before the gates of excellence, the high gods have placed sweat."

The following June, William Armstrong retired after a fifty-two year career teaching at Kent.

As the twenty-first century approached with its increasing emphasis on technology, Kent continued to look forward and to grow and meet its challenges. In 1995, Kent and twenty-nine other schools became part of the Anytime

Clockwise from top left: Soccer; Neither Red Sox nor Yankees—it's Kent!; Boys varsity lacrosse; Night basketball games are a feature of the winter term.

Anywhere Learning Program, initiated by Microsoft and Toshiba. This was an innovative program in which every student and teacher would be provided with a laptop computer. Computer technology had first come to Kent in 1966 when Kent became a member of the General Electric Time-Shared Computer System. At that time a tele-typewriter was installed in the math office through which contact could be made with a General Electric 235 Computer in Valley Forge, Pennsylvania. At first, the machine was used in connection with a course in math, but it was hoped that other departments would eventually find a use for it, too. Now, some thirty years later, technology was an important part of daily academic life. Students took their laptops to class, using them to write papers, to create Power Point presentations, and, eventually, as the entire campus was wired, to do research on the Internet from their classrooms and dorm rooms as well as from the library and the technology classroom. An intra-school Local Area Network (LAN) was created, with connections in every dorm room, telephones in every room, and connection to the Internet by a T1 line. In the next few years, the Kentranet, an in-house network, made it possible for almost everything that had been in print—attendance lists, class assignments, calendars—to be accessible by computer. Most of the School's daily business was carried on by e-mail or by various programs written by Kent faculty to meet the specific needs of the School; attendance was reported, grades and comments were written and sent to the Studies Office, information about students, including their pictures, could be accessed with the click of a mouse. Perhaps for the students Instant Messaging was one of the most important advances as it became the way to communicate with friends near (even in the next room) and far. By 2006, most of the School had wireless access, so they could even conduct their computer business sitting outside under the trees if they wished.

In the summer of 1995 the Summer Academic Camp held its first sessions, designed for junior high students. Forty-two students, ages 11 to 14, from ten states and two foreign countries embarked on an exploration of creative writing. The schedule included various extracurricular activities, sports, and social events, and at the end of the two-week-long camp everyone agreed that Kent's newest venture was a huge success. The camp has grown in the years since, running from early July to the end of the month. Students enjoy

WILLIAM H. ARMSTRONG

William H. Armstrong arrived at Kent in 1944 from his beloved Shenandoah Valley and taught here for more than fifty years, instilling in his students the notion that nothing in life which is worth anything comes easy, but rather through hard work. He titled his first book on study skills *Study is Hard Work*, a title which scares modern editors with its bold affirmation that the business of being a student is not easy and that there are no short cuts. His editor at Harper's was bold, too, and the book sallied forth from the valley of the Housatonic to proclaim its assertions and guide students for generations in their attempts to master their subjects in school. Many alumni of Kent remember it well and reflect on the impact in their lives of this remarkable man and his stern admonitions about effort.

Bill had two characteristics which made him a dynamic teacher: charisma and an utter devotion to his students and his subject. Bill insisted that his students learn how to manage their time, learn how to listen, learn how to identify what was important in learning and in life, and learn to be self-sufficient. He lived his life according to the very principles he espoused, becoming in the process one of the most fundamentally honest teachers at the School. He also knew how to tell a good tale, how to deliver a dramatic declamation, when to say a proper word of condemnation or encouragement to a student, when to offer a pithy quotation,

Bill Armstrong delivered the Prize Day address in 1991.

and in general how to make his class memorable.

Generations of students grasped the honesty in Bill's way of life and tried their best to live up to that standard, whether they were grappling with the Peloponnesian War, filling out their planbooks, or polishing windows while working off their hours. And all, with great delight, related stories to one another of his exploits in class, his oft-expressed love of the natural world, and his astonishing self-reliance.

For all his apparent simplicity, Bill was a complex man and gave each of us only a glimpse of the whole of his personality and achievements. As the historian Shelby Foote has said of another great Virginian, one can say of Bill: As you talk with him "he will smile and give you with unflinching courtesy . . . letters . . . and photographs, kindness . . . and advice, and do it with such grace and gentleness that you will know you have the whole of him pinned down, mapped out easy to understand, and so you have. All things except the heart; the heart he kept a secret to the end from all the picklocks of biographers" (*Kent Quarterly*, Spring 1999).

Bill Armstrong was a man of many talents. He built his own house on the hill he named Kimadee for his three children, Kip, Mary, and David; he dug his own swimming pool; he raised sheep; and he planted the hillside with daffodils. He was an early riser, using the wee hours of the morning to read the Bible, Chaucer, Shakespeare. And he loved the natural world. His students remember him for his strictness, but they also recall being taken on nature walks to find warblers in the springtime. The literary world remembers Bill, too, for he was the author of the novel *Sounder*, which received the 1970 John Newbery Medal for "the most distinguished contribution to literature for children published in 1969" and which when made into a movie was nominated for an Oscar—unfortunately in the same year that *The Godfather* was nominated. He was also a painter, who captured the world around him on canvas. But Bill was an artist in other ways, too, a man who saw the world around him as the work of an even greater artist, and who cherished that world, sharing his love for it with countless generations of Kent students and with all who knew him.

Above: Construction of the Kent Early Learning Center.

all sorts of activities, sports, arts, and trips to interesting places in the area. Not only has the Camp introduced youngsters to boarding school life, it has also brought some of them to Kent as full-time students.

In 1998 Kent School opened its own Day Care Center, west of the campus on Macedonia Road. The building was designed by S/L/A/M, the designers of the new buildings on the consolidated campus. While the center was primarily intended for faculty children, it was also available to townspeople on a space-available basis. So, as the older members of the Kent community worked on Power Point presentations, wrote essays on their laptops, and surfed the Internet, the youngest members of the Kent community, town and gown, worked away with crayons and paste and paper.

The consolidated campus attracted students who might not have considered Kent when the School was on two campuses. While the School had been a pioneer in its decision to enroll girls in the first place, it had fallen behind competitively in the years that its sister schools had become fully coeducational. Now Kent, too, enjoyed the renewed energy and intellectual ferment that consolidation had brought to the Valley. Leadership was shared equally by boys and girls. Two senior prefects, two vergers, two sacristans, two dining hall stewards, two library proctors, two Blue Key heads and the various dorm prefects helped to run the school. *The Kent News* for most of those early years on one campus had two editors-in-chief, a boy and a girl. Responsibility was shared, and the girls quickly became an integral part of the valley, no longer visitors of a sort. The benefits were clear in other areas, too. As interest in the School and the number of applications for admission increased, so, too, did the academic quality of the student body as evidenced in the number of students admitted to top tier colleges and universities. New languages were added to the curriculum, first, for a few years, Japanese, replaced, after careful consideration,

Below: The tapping ceremony for the class of 2006.

by Mandarin Chinese. The arts, always part of the curriculum, took on new life. Kent musicians participated in competitions all over New England, and Kent artists took home prizes on a regular basis. A string orchestra grew from four or five players to a full string orchestra and frequently those players joined the concert band in a full concert orchestra. Singers not only found success at Kent but went on to professional careers in music. Theater flourished and, again, Kent graduates went on to study the various aspects of theater in college. A Math Team was started and before

long it was winning competitions in which it was pitted against the best schools in New England. A new vitality was apparent in every area of School life as Kent celebrated the turn of the century and a new millennium.

The twenty-first century brought changes and challenges to Kent and to the world. No one will forget that dreadful day, September 11, 2001, when two hijacked airplanes were flown into the twin towers of the World Trade Center in New York, another was flown into the Pentagon, and a fourth crashed in Pennsylvania when passengers fought to keep it from its goal somewhere in Washington, DC. It was a Tuesday, the second

Above and below: Music and drama are an important part of Kent life.

Photo by Erin Reilly '08.

day of classes, and Kent students and faculty first heard of the attack in Chapel, when Father Schell announced to the congregation that two commercial aircraft flying from Boston to Los Angeles had crashed into the World Trade Center shortly before 9 AM. The congregation then joined in prayer for the victims of the tragedy and for the nation, leaving the chapel in silence. Kent students, faculty, and staff shared their grief as they watched the devastation on television, and faculty members were in the library helping students whose family members were thought to be in the area of the World Trade towers and the Pentagon. At the end of the academic day, the community gathered in the Dining Hall for an update from Father Schell and to pray for those who had died, among them, we later learned, several members of the Kent Family. Nothing would ever be quite the same. However, in spite of threats of terrorism and war, once again, in far-off places that suddenly in the twenty-first century were not so far off, Kent stood firm. A Day of Service and Remembrance followed almost immediately. After a brief service in the chapel, students and faculty went out into surrounding communities to paint, wash fire trucks and ambulances, clean up playing fields and public spaces, and serve food in homeless shelters—to serve others. On the first anniversary of the attack, the School again held a day of service projects after gathering in the chapel to pray and share their thoughts. In the five years since 9/11, community service, always an aspect of Kent life, has become even more important as organizations like REACH, Habitat for Humanity, and the My Soldier Club, annual blood drives, and various initiatives to meet specific needs such as the devastation after Hurricane Katrina in 2005 have engaged the School in ongoing service to others outside the School itself.

Also, in the months that followed, Kent welcomed a series of speakers on various aspects of war, terrorism, and national security. In October, Serge Schmemann '63, Pulitzer Prize winning journalist at the *New York Times*, shared his thoughts about September 11. Later, in December, James Hoge, Jr., editor of *Foreign Affairs*, discussed the state of world affairs in the aftermath of the attack.

KENT'S PULITZER PRIZE WINNERS

Kent takes great pride in the four alumni who have been honored with Pulitzer Prizes, one of them, Roger Sessions '11, twice.

Roger Sessions '11.

Roger Sessions '11 was one of America's best known composers in the 20th century. Sessions began to take piano lessons when he was 4 and had begun to compose music by the time he was 12. He entered Harvard at 14 and later studied at Yale. An educator as well as a composer, he taught at Boston University, Smith, Princeton, UC Berkeley, and the Juilliard School of Music in New York City. He was universally admired and respected and was honored many times, receiving several Guggenheim Fellowships and a Carnegie Fellowship, the Prix de Rome, and an honorary doctorate from Harvard. In 1974 he received a special Pulitzer citation for his life's work, and in 1982 he was awarded the Pulitzer Prize in Music for his "Concerto for Orchestra," his final work.

Robert S. Hillyer '13.

Robert S. Hillyer '13, best known to generations of Kent students and faculty as the composer of the words of the School Song, won the Pulitzer Prize in 1934 for his Collected Verse. At the time of his death he was professor of English at the University of Delaware. His widow established the Robert S. Hillyer '13 Prize in English, first awarded in 1974 to Sara Laschever and most recently to Augusta Binns-Berkey '06. Hillyer's Ode written on the occasion of Kent's fiftieth anniversary opens this book and provides the chapter titles.

James Gould Cozzens '22.

James Gould Cozzens '22 was a prolific novelist, acclaimed by the critics. His most popular novel was probably *By Love Possessed*, which was made into a movie starring Lana Turner. He won the Pulitzer Prize in Fiction in 1949 for his 1948 novel *Guard of Honor*. His collection of stories, *Children and Others*, is largely based on his experiences at Kent under the guidance of Father Sill. Cozzens told a reporter "Kent marked me for life. If there is hard work to be done and I get out of it, I feel extremely guilty."

Kent's most recent Pulitzer honoree is Serge Schmemann '63. Mr. Schmemann, the former bureau chief for the *New York Times* in Bonn, won the 1991 Pulitzer Prize for International Reporting for his coverage of the reunification of Germany. Mr. Schmemann served as bureau chief for the New York Times in Moscow, Bonn, and Jerusalem before his present position as editorial page editor of the International *Herald Tribune*. In 1997 he published his memoirs, *Echoes of a Native Land: Two Centuries of a Russian Village*, based on the his grandparents' home village near Kaluga.

Photo of Sessions from www.presser.com/composers/info, the website for Theodore Presser Company. Photo of Cozzens from The New York Times Book Review, *August 2, 1964.*

Third in the series was former director of the CIA, James Woolsey, and fourth was Professor Donald Kagan, Hillhouse Professor of History and Classics at Yale University, whose topic was Liberal Education and Patriotism. The final speaker in the series was Robert D. Kaplan, contributing editor of *The Atlantic Monthly*. In 2003, the Cyrus Vance '35 Lectures were established, bringing well-known experts on international affairs to the campus.

In answer, perhaps, to the divisions caused by terrorism Kent became even more international. From the beginning, the School had welcomed students from other countries, first from England, then soon after World War I from Germany, later from Korea and Japan and other Asian countries. But after September 11,

2001, thanks to the generosity and the vision of a friend of Kent, Henry Kravis, Kent welcomed some students from the Middle East and Afghanistan. For eighteen months the School made strenuous efforts throughout the region from Morocco to Afghanistan to identify potential students, using its educational network, the State Department, the British government, churches and camps, and the Institute for International Education (Fulbright Committees). Kent now has contacts throughout the Middle East who are on the lookout for good candidates for Kent. The Habbi Scholarships—and the opportunity that they represent—have been well received despite the peer pressure on young people to remain at home in familiar surroundings. A unique description of Kent is that it is a school where a Jewish philanthropist provides scholarships for Muslims from the Middle East at an Episcopal Church school in Connecticut. In the 2005-2006 year, Kent's 100th year, the student body included students from Thailand, Afghanistan, Palestine, Germany, China, Korea, Canada, Turkey, Latvia, Croatia, Spain, France, Jamaica, the Bahamas, Brazil, Austria, Poland, Saudi Arabia, Ukraine, Taiwan, Mexico, Guatemala, Scotland, Nigeria, the Philippines, and Haiti. This diversity is preparing Kent students for life in the global community in which they will be leaders.

In the first years of the twenty-first century, the physical permanent Kent continued to grow also. The football field sprouted lights in the fall of 2001, dedicated in memory of Jean Theobald, wife of football coach Cy Theobald, and on Friday, September 28, 2001, students, teachers, parents, and alumni cheered the varsity football team on to a 42-9 victory over Trinity-Pawling in the first-ever nighttime football game at Kent. Later, in 2002, Middle Dorm was enlarged when Borsdorff Hall was built on the east side of the building, facing the river.

The next three years saw this growth continue as the Benjamin Waring

Below: A triumphant Kent wins the Spoon Game against Loomis.

Partridge Rowing Center was built at the Skiff Mountain Road entrance to the School, and further up the road a new complex of seven faculty houses was constructed.

As part of Father Schell's plan to make Kent the best School it could be, in October 2002 Father Schell and the Board of Trustees announced the Campaign for the Permanent Kent, the largest fund-raising campaign in the history of the School. The goal was $75,000,000. When the campaign ended in June 2005, the total had reached just over $80,000,000. As a result scholarship

WILLIAM BERLE BORSDORFF '35

William Berle Borsdorff loved Kent. In his five years as a student he was a dutiful, hard-working young man, enthusiastic in everything both in and out of class that he set his mind and heart to: from football and ice hockey to baseball and band. He was a fervent team player, devoted to his senior prefect, Cy Vance, and to his masters and to Father Sill. He loved the chapel, and in letters and conversations over the years he said that in St. Joseph's walls "I found the compass with which to guide my way through life." Through his participation in the Kent experience of study, work, play, and prayer, Bill came to embrace its Founder's motto: Simplicity of Life, Directness of Purpose, and Self-Reliance.

Throughout his life, at Kent and Dartmouth College, during his service in World War II, over his long and distinguished career with Johnson & Johnson Company and Jelco Laboratories International, and in his devotion to family and friends, Bill was remarkable in how very well he lived both his Episcopal faith and his beloved School's motto.

Bill was characteristically modest and self-effacing with regard both to his own accomplishments and to his care for and service to others. Yet, for all his modesty, how brightly he shone and continues to shine in the lives of the people and places he loved.

After his death in February 2004, at the opening of its winter meeting, the board of trustees passed a Resolution of Thanks:

"Whereas William Berle Borsdorff '35

"Was an exemplary five-year student at Kent and an accomplished graduate of Dartmouth and The Amos Tuck School of Business;

"Served his country with distinction in WWII as a PT Boat Commander and was awarded the U.S. Navy Silver Star and the French Croix de Guerre with Bronze Star;

"Accomplished a noteworthy 30-year career with Johnson & Johnson, culminating in his Presidency of Jelco Laboratories International;

"Whereas:

"He registered 68 years of unbroken support of the Annual Alumni Fund and was a member of both the Bell Tower Society and the K-E-Y Society;

"He sought, by the example of his giving, to transform and elevate our sense of the possible, making over $8 million in planned and outright gifts to endow a Teaching Chair, scholarship aid, and his own annual giving; to fund a biology laboratory in Dickinson Science Center; to fund a new wing of Middle Dorm; and to provide funds for two new faculty homes;

"Whereas:

"For these and other services to the School he was made Kent School's first Honorary Trustee and an Honorary chairman of The Campaign for The Permanent Kent; Be it Resolved That:

"The Board of Trustees hereby offers thanks for the life of William Berle Borsdorff '35 and registers its appreciation for the inspiration he provided through his giving in an effort to make 'Kent School the best darn School in New England.'"

William B. Borsdorff '35 with Father Schell.

aid was increased, and by the end of the Campaign eighteen endowed faculty chairs had been established.

Just as a young man with vision and energy and faith had succeeded in founding his school on the banks of the Housatonic in 1906, so another young man had taken up the challenge in 1981 and with vision and energy had led the School into the next century and to the centennial of its founding. In February 2006, Richardson W. Schell was honored as Chief Executive of the Year by the Council for Advancement and Support of Education (CASE) at their annual conference and awards ceremony in Montreal, Quebec. CASE defines the Award, which was established in 2005 to honor institutional leaders for their outstanding contributions to their campus communities, for efforts promoting public understanding of education, and for support of advancement on their campuses. "Awardees must have demonstrated the ability to increase their institution's stature in the community and to establish a positive image for their institution while leading it to even higher levels of success."

In her tribute to Father Schell, Patricia Jackson, Vice President for Advancement at Smith College, said:

"This year's recipient, the Reverend Richardson W. Schell, has sustained an incredible level of excellence and commitment for 25 years as the headmaster and rector of Kent School in Kent, Connecticut. A friend described Father Schell in the following manner: 'He is old-fashioned in the best sense, in that his principal desire has always been to empower the formation of human beings. Everyone who serves with him or under him will attest to his amazing heart for the young, and to his ability to inspire others to more authentic

Above: (Left) The Benjamin Waring Partridge Rowing Center. (Right) The faculty village on Skiff Mountain Road.

Below: (Top) A home in the faculty village. (Bottom) The house that used to be on Chapel Hill before the Rectory, with the diamond-shaped windows from old St. Joseph's Chapel.

FACULTY ENDOWED CHAIRS

For many years, the Independence Foundation Chair was the main method of honoring outstanding members of the Kent faculty. Henry Syer was the first person so honored. Those honored held the chair for three years.

Henry Syer	1967
O.B. Davis	1970
Bill Armstrong	1973
Coe DeVillafranca	1977
Hal Bredberg	1982
Charles Genovese	1985
George Ludlow	1988
John Newton	1991
Robert Mott	2000
Joel Kelly	2003
Loretto Roney	2006

In 2001 the first endowed teaching chair at Kent was established by Judith B. and Howard B. Wentz, Jr. Many more followed and the number continues to grow.

Thomas K. Roney	The Judith B. and Howard B. Wentz, Jr. Teaching Chair in Interdisciplinary Studies
Joan M. Beattie	The William B. Borsdorff 1935 Teaching Chair in English
O.B. Davis '42	The O.B. Davis '42 Teaching Chair in English
Donald K. Gowan '66	The H. Alexander Salm '37 Teaching Chair in American History
Jennifer M. Lynch	The Robert F. Hoerle '52 Teaching Chair in the Arts
Edward C. Dunn	The William A. Howland '32 World War II Memorial Teaching Chair in History
Linda B. Perkins	The David C. Clapp '56 Teaching Chair in English
Peter H. Goodwin	The Hadley Case '29 Teaching Chair in the Physical Sciences
Charles B. Emerich	The Centennial Teaching Chair in Music
Marel D'Orbessan Rogers '65	The William B. Armstrong (Hon)'48 Teaching Chair in General Studies
John S. Perkins	The Brophy Teaching Chair in Mathematics
Curtis Scofield Lisa Brody	The Arthur Collins '48 Teaching Chair in Art & Architecture
Anne O'Keeffe Russell Jennifer M. Hobbs	The Class of 2000 Teaching Chair
Barbara Friedman Stout '66 John R. Hinman, Jr.	The Class of 2001 Teaching Chair
Dr. Ann Yumin Meng Bonnie S. Kerr	The Harlan W. and Ria S. Newell '36 Teaching Chair in Modern Languages
Randall J. Hobbs Stephen J. Robey, Jr.	The Norman Scott, Jr. '40 Teaching Chair in Physics

and competent lives as servant-leaders in our society—students and teachers alike.' . . .

"At the age of 30, he took on the daunting task of heading the largest Episcopal Church Boarding School in the United States. From the outset, he was a hands-on headmaster in all phases of school life, continuing to teach and leading as rector while assuming new duties with the board, alumni, and friends of the school. Early on, Father Schell's priority was to get the school into the black operationally. This took him three years, and it led to the realization that for the school to survive long-term it would need to consolidate its two campuses into one and streamline its operations. This was undertaken in 1986, and more than $65 million worth of construction took place between 1990 and 1996.

Above: The Case Award.

"To help finance this effort, Father Schell established a model since followed by many other schools when he secured $26 million in tax-exempt bond funding, while also garnering more than $20 million in private funds.

"More recently, between 1998 and 2005, Father Schell led the $75 million Campaign for the Permanent Kent to secure endowment funding in support of faculty and scholarship aid.

"$80.1 million was raised.

"As a result of this Campaign, 18 Teaching Chairs were established, average faculty salaries were raised significantly, financial aid resources greatly increased.

"Kent now enjoys a burgeoning popularity and greatly increased selectivity, with 80 percent of last year's senior class gaining entry at first-and second-tier colleges and universities.

Below: St. Joseph's Chapel in Kent's 100th year.

"Former U.S. Secretary of State Henry A. Kissinger, a long-time resident of Kent, recently wrote: 'I have witnessed with pride the school's growth academically . . . the recruitment of top-rate instructors and enhancement to all areas of faculty life.'

"He adds that: '[Father Schell's] vision, dedication, and hands-on leadership have had an extraordinary impact on Kent School, and he is an educator who truly embodies the spirit and principles of the Chief Executive Leadership Award.' . . .

"For his untiring philanthropy, his wide-reaching leadership and a depth of vision that enabled him to transform his institution over 25

Right: The first page of the score of "Bright Auroral Skies," commissioned for the Centennial.

CENTENNIAL PROCLAMATION

WHEREAS Father Frederick Herbert Sill O.H.C. had the vision in 1906 humbly yet purposefully to found his Kent School in a converted farmhouse on the banks of the Housatonic River and bring a quality, church-centered education to boys from families of modest means;

WHEREAS this School community has since applied that farming tradition in a new way by faithfully adhering to its motto of Simplicity of Life, Directness of Purpose, and Self-Reliance, tilling the fields of knowledge in the minds of its youth, planting them with the seeds of character, and nurturing in them the growth of potential;

WHEREAS Kent School in 1960 took the lead among independent boarding schools in extending the benefits of its mission to girls;

WHEREAS the unstinting dedication of ten decades of Kent faculty and staff and the varied accomplishments and unflagging support of over 10,000 graduates and their parents have not only validated the worth of the Kent experience but also affirmed the School's determination to remain a leader in secondary education for a long time to come;

BE IT THEREFORE RESOLVED THAT with this third day of June 2006 we who take pride in Kent's past, who rejoice in its present, and who espouse hope for its future do hereby proclaim the commencement of Kent School's Centennial Celebration year that will end on June 17th of Alumni Reunion Weekend 2007.

Temperantia, Fiducia, Constantia.

years, CASE District I is proud to recognize the Reverend Richardson W. Schell with the 2006 Chief Executive Leadership Award."

In the history of the world, one hundred years is a mere eye-blink, but in the life of an institution such as Kent, in which generations are measured in four-year spans, one hundred years is twenty-five generations of students, young men and, after 1960, young women who enter as young teenagers, most of them away from home for the first time, and who leave as confident young adults. It is an awesome responsibility for those to whom these lives are entrusted, and much of the strength of Kent depends on the men and women who, like Chaucer's Oxford Clerk, "gladly lerne and gladly teche." Six headmasters and hundreds of teachers, supported by the countless members of the staff who take care of the School in all its aspects, thousands of parents, numerous members of the board of trustees, and today thousands of alumni/ ae, have all shared the responsibility for making Father Sill's dream of the permanent Kent a reality—a living, growing School.

And so, Kent has reached its 100th year. From its beginning in Clarence Fuller's farmhouse, Kent has been growing and changing and in that process becoming more itself. Father Sill had $200 and a dream. Kent today is the realization of that dream. It will continue to evolve, to move into the future with a sense of commitment to the intellectual and spiritual education of young men and women who are preparing to take their place in an uncertain future. Kent stands proudly among the great schools.

Above: Kyle Beek '08 and Courtney Daukas '09 read the Proclamation declaring the official beginning of Kent's Centennial Celebration on June 3, 2006.

Centennial

Fear not the autumn, for you
shall find life here is simple.
Embraced by the memories
of a hundred years past,
greeted by the warm tradition
of those who came before you,
you shall discover your purpose.
Direct, yet full of possibility, life
in Algo's peaceful shadow shall
make clear what was once blinding.
Rely not on others, but on yourself,
and the gift of enlightenment
will be yours.

Fear not the summer, for now
you are ready. Know that earned
accomplishments will carry you far.
Celebrate your years in this
lovely valley land, as the nostalgia
you once admired has inherited you
till dawn and darkness are no more.

Temperantia, Fiducia, Constantia—100 years

—Benjamin Louis Seidenstein '07

KENT SCHOOL

TEMPERANTIA FIDUCIA CONSTANTIA

CENTENNIAL

Top: The Processional. Bottom: The Reverend Peter G. Cheney, Executive Director of the National Association of Episcopal Schools, preached at the Centennial Eucharist. Right: Headmaster Richardson W. Schell '69.

KENT

One Hundred Years—And One Memorable Weekend in October

THE HIGHLIGHT OF KENT'S YEARLONG CELEBRATION TOOK place on Centennial Weekend, October 20–21, 2006, including a series of events and generations of participants. Marel d'Orbessan Rogers, director of the John Gray Park Library and member of the class of 1965, headed the committee that worked for more than a year to plan the festivities.

Celebration of the Holy Eucharist began the Friday evening commemoration. Hundreds of students, parents, faculty, administrators, alumni and friends, including two members of The Order of Holy Cross, filled St. Joseph's Chapel, where the altar was adorned with a new frontal created especially for the anniversary. Eleven priests joined the processional and participated in the event, including the celebrant, The Right Reverend E. Don Taylor, Vicar Bishop of the Episcopal Diocese of New York and The Reverend Peter G. Cheney, executive director of the National Association of Episcopal Schools, who delivered the sermon. During Communion those in attendance enjoyed the premier of "Now thank we all our God," composed and conducted by faculty member Thomas Holcombe and performed by the Kent School Chamber Choir.

Then, more than 600 guests processed down Chapel Road to a transformed Springs Center, location for the Centennial Dinner. Flowing gray curtains festooned with hand-tied blue bows surrounded the space, creating a festive atmosphere for the celebrants. A birthday cake crowned with sparklers served as a centerpiece on each table. After addresses by President of the Board of Trustees, Brandon Sweitzer '60 and Headmaster Dick Schell '69, the Kent Orchestra and Chorus, led by faculty member Charles Emerich, brought the crowd to its feet with the spectacular musical premier of "Bright Auroral Skies." The piece by American composer Robert Shelton was commissioned especially for Kent's Centennial. As guests finished dinner, the birthday cake sparklers were lighted, symbolizing the excitement and pride that energized the room throughout the evening.

Saturday's events began with the Centennial Lecture given by acclaimed author Edmund Morris, Pulitzer Prize-winning biographer of Theodore Roosevelt and Ronald Reagan. Morris contrasted life in 1906 with today, providing a historical perspective on the country in the year of Kent's founding. Following a buffet luncheon, visitors had many choices, from taking a tour of campus, to watching a soccer or football game, to attending the Hill Campus tea at the Marvelwood School, Kent's girls' campus from 1963–1992.

—Julie Vecchitto

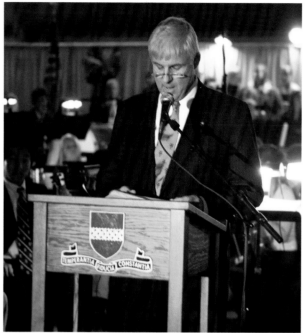

Counterclockwise from top left: The Right Reverend E. Don Taylor, Vicar Bishop of the Episcopal Diocese of New York; Brandon Sweitzer '60, chairman of the board of trustees, welcomed guests; The Centennial Frontal; Tents were set up next to the Springs Center for the reception following the Centennial Eucharist and preceding the dinner.

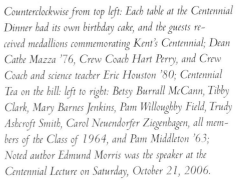

Counterclockwise from top left: Each table at the Centennial Dinner had its own birthday cake, and the guests received medallions commemorating Kent's Centennial; Dean Cathe Mazza '76, Crew Coach Hart Perry, and Crew Coach and science teacher Eric Houston '80; Centennial Tea on the hill: left to right: Betsy Burrall McCann, Tibby Clark, Mary Barnes Jenkins, Pam Willoughby Field, Trudy Ashcroft Smith, Carol Neuendorfer Ziegenhagen, all members of the Class of 1964, and Pam Middleton '63; Noted author Edmund Morris was the speaker at the Centennial Lecture on Saturday, October 21, 2006.

1906 ⚜ KENT CENTENNIAL ⚜ 2006

APPENDIX

2006–2007 KENT SCHOOL FACULTY

Richardson W. Schell '69 (1980)
A.B. Harvard College, M.Div. Yale University,
D.Litt. (Hon.) Keimyung University
Headmaster and Rector

Joan M. Beattie (1988)
B.A. University of Massachusetts, M.A. Columbia
University, M.Litt. Middlebury College
English Department Chair
The William B. Borsdorff '35 Teaching Chair in English

Kristin C. Benjamin (1997)
B.A. Middlebury College, M.A. Tufts University
French

Michael A. Benjamin (2001)
B.A. Middlebury College, M.S. Yale University
Science

Ashton Betancourt (2005)
A.B. Yale University
Mathematics

Timothy Booth (1998)
B.A. Hamilton College
History

Lisa Brody (1992)
B.A., B.F.A. University of Pennsylvania
Art
The Arthur Collins '48 Teaching Chair in Art and Architecture

Timothy J. Carey (2003)
B.A. Yale University
Theology

Oliviya Chavka (2002)
B.A. Uzghorod State University
French

Bettina P. Cloutier (1994)
B.A. New England College
Assistant Dean of Students

Marc L. Cloutier (1981)
B.S. Southern Connecticut State University
Director of Development, French

Kenneth Corey, Ph.D. (2002)
B.S. University of Massachusetts, M.S., Ph.D. North Carolina State University
Science

Joel A. Danisi, M.D. (1985)
B.S. SUNY Stony Brook, M.D. Medical College of Virginia,
American Board Certified, Internal Medicine 1985
School Physician

Elizabeth B. Davis (2001)
B.A. Kenyon College
History

Otis Benson Davis '42 (1949)
A.B. Princeton University, M.A. Johns Hopkins University
Senior Master, English
The O. B. Davis '42 Teaching Chair in English

Robert DesMarais, Jr. (1989)
B.A. Trinity College
Classics Department Chair

Robert A. Diehl (2006)
B.A. Wesleyan University
Math, Psychology

Edward Conaway Dunn (1984)
B.A. Columbia University, M.A.T. Teachers College, Columbia University
History
The William A. H. Howland '32 WWII Memorial Chair in History

Charles B. Emerich (1981)
B.S. West Chester State College, M.Ed. Pennsylvania State University
Music Department Chair
The Centennial Teaching Chair in Music

Krista Falcone (2005)
B.A. College of the Holy Cross
English

Adam W. Fischer (1998)
B.A. Columbia College
Director of Technology

Ryan Foote (2006)
B.A. Vassar College, MAT Brown University

Kendra L. Galusha (1996)
B.A. Houghton College
Mathematics

Daniel R. Genck '01 (2005)
B.A. College of St. Benedict and St John's University
English, Assistant Dean of Students

Peter H. Goodwin (1973)
B.A. Middlebury College, M.A. Trinity College
Science Department Chair
The Hadley Case '29 Teaching Chair in the Physical Sciences

Susan Roome Goodwin '69 (1985)
B.A. Wellesley College
Science

Donald K. Gowan '66 (1970)
B.A. University of North Carolina
History Department Chair
The H. Alexander Salm '37 Teaching Chair in American History

David P. Greene, Ph.D. (2000)
B.A. M.Phil., Ph.D. Syracuse, C.T.S. Episcopal Divinity
School, M.T.S. Texas Christian University
Theology Department Chair

Laura K. Herr (2005)
B.A., B.A. University of Michigan, J.D. American University
History

Matthew G. Herr (2005)
B.A. University of Michigan, MBA University of Phoenix
History, Psychology

Kristelle A. Hicks (2005)
B.A. Bates College
Spanish

John R. Hinman, Jr. (1992)
B.A. Rutgers University, M.A. University of Virginia
English
The Class of 2001 Teaching Chair

Jennifer Malone Hobbs (1994)
A.B. Bowdoin College, M.A. University of Connecticut
Music
The Class of 2000 Teaching Chair

Randall J. Hobbs (1993)
B.S. Dartmouth College
Science
The Norman Scott, Jr. '40 Teaching Chair in Physics

Thomas W. Holcombe (1977)
A.B. Harvard College, M.S.M., M.Div. Union Theological Seminary
Music

Barbara A. Houston (1983)
B.A. Wheaton College
History

Eric L. Houston '80 (1984)
B.S. Trinity College
Science

Thomas A. Hunt (2003)
B.A. Syracuse University
English

Elizabeth A. Jakupciak (2002)
B.A. Augustana College, J.D. Hamline School of Law
Mathematics

Isabel A. Janelli (2005)
B.A. Middlebury College
Spanish

Joel G. Kelly (1965)
A.B. Harvard College
Classics Department Chair, Emeritus; Secretary to the Faculty, Emeritus
The Independence Foundation Chair

John S. Kerr (1970)
A.B. Kenyon College, M.A. Middlebury College
Director of Planned Giving

Jesse W. Klingebiel (1994)
B.S. Bucknell University, M.S. University of New Hampshire
Science, Associate Director of Admissions

Steven Krueger, Ph.D. (2000)
B.A. Loyola Marymount College, M.A. Ruprecht-Karls-University
Heidelberg, M.A. Dalhousie University, Ph.D. Oxford University
German

John H. Lintner (1999)
B.A. Middlebury College, M.A. Middlebury
College, J.D. University of Connecticut
College Guidance

Jennifer M. Lynch (1996)
B.A. Connecticut College, M.A. New York University
Art Department Chair, Assistant Chaplain
The Robert F. Hoerle '52 Teaching Chair in the Arts

James C. MacLeod (1982)
B.S. University of Delaware, M.A.T. Trenton State College
Mathematics

Margaret Magee (2002)
B.A. Bowdoin College
Science

Paul A. Mantegani (1981)
B.A. Bowdoin College
History

Todd Marble (1992)
B.A. Colby College, M.A. Trinity College
Director of Athletics and Student Activities

Catherine M. Mazza '76 (1981)
B.A. Marietta College, M.A. Boston University
Dean of Students

Mary S. McDonald (2004)
B.A. University of Georgia, M.A. University of Western Georgia
College Guidance

Joseph D. McDonough (2006)
B.A. Williams College
Classics

Ann Yumin Meng, Ed.D. (2004)
B.A., M.Ed. Beijing Capitol Normal University, B.A. Beijing
University, M.Ed., Ed.D, University of Massachusetts
Chinese
The Harlan and Ria S. Newell '36 Teaching Chair in Modern Languages

Jesse Minneman (2006)
A.B. Bowdoin College
History

Karen Moreno (1997)
B.A. University of Northern Iowa, M.A. Western Connecticut
State University, M.S. Southern Connecticut State University
English/ESL

Ben Nadire, Ph.D. (1997)
M.S. University of Montpelier, Ph.D. Northeastern University
Mathematics

Robert F. Ober III (1991)
B.A. Rollins College, M.A.L.S. Wesleyan University
History

Linda B. Perkins (1969)
B.A. Colby College, M.A. University of New Hampshire
English
The David C. Clapp '56 Teaching Chair in English

John S. Perkins (1969)
B.A. Colby College, M.A. University of New Hampshire
Mathematics
The Brophy Teaching Chair in Mathematics

Amy J. Raskind (2003)
B.S. Union College, M.A. University of Colorado, Denver
School Counselor

Stephen J. Robey, Jr. (1993)
B.S. United States Military Academy, M.Ed. University of Hartford
Science
The Norman Scott '40 Teaching Chair in Physics

Marel D'Orbessan Rogers '65 (1985)
A.B. Brown University, M.S.L.S. Simmons College
Director of Library, Third Form Seminar, Secretary to the Faculty
The William H. Armstrong Teaching Chair in General Studies

Servane Rogers (2001)
M.A. Université de Paris – La Sorbonne, M.A. Washington University
French, Spanish

Loretto S. Roney (1978)
B.S. Trinity College, M.A. University of Vermont
Academic Dean, Mathematics
The Independence Foundation Chair

Thomas K. Roney (1971)
A.B. St. Michael's College, M.A. University of Vermont
Mathematics Department Chair
The Judith B. and Howard B. Wentz, Jr. Teaching
Chair in Interdisciplinary Studies

Sara G. Ross (2006)
B.A. Middlebury College, M.S. Lesley University
College Guidance

Bjorn W. Runquist (1977)
B.A. Colgate University, M.A. Kings College, University of London
Modern Languages Department Chair, French

Anne K. O'Keeffe Russell (1990)
A.B. Princeton University, M.A. University of Georgia
Classics
Dean of Faculty

Juan G. Sanchez (2006)
B.S. Central Connecticut State University
Spanish

Kevin R. Saxton (2003)
A.B. Bowdoin College
Mathematics

Andrew H. Schneider '00 (2004)
B.A. Rutgers University
English, Writing Lab

Curtis Scofield (1990)
B.F.A. Alfred University; M.F.A. Kent State University
Art
The Arthur Collins '48 Teaching Chair in Art and Architecture

Cheryl D. Setchell (2006)
B.A. Colgate University
History

Jonathon L. Shoop (2006)
B.S. University of Wisconsin-Eau Claire, M.S.
University of Wisconsin-Oshkosh
Mathematics

Thomas B. Sides (1989)
A.B. Bowdoin College; Diploma, University of
Wisconsin Graduate School of Banking
Business Manager

Garrison Smith (2004)
B.A. Yale University
Science

Jeremy P. Sokolnicki (2003)
B.A. Hamilton College
Science, Assistant Dean of Students

Geoffrey Stewart (2003)
B.A. University of Rochester, M.A. Northwestern University
English

Barbara Friedman Stout '66 (1973)
B.A. Earlham College, M.A. Northwestern University
English
The Class of 2001 Teaching Chair

Kathryn F. Sullivan '94 (2001)
B.S. Syracuse University
Director of Admissions

John A. Torrez (2005)
B.S. Texas A & M
Spanish

Catherine A. Tynan (2006)
B.A. Colby College, M.F.A. Warren Wilson College
English

Julie L. Veremey (2005)
B.A. Brown University
Science

Jonathan A. Voorhees (2004)
B.A. University of California, Santa Cruz, M.Div.
Church Divinity School of the Pacific
Chaplain, Theology, English

Wayne Walton (2003)
B.A. Ithaca College
Assistant Dean of Students

Jessica B. Watkin (2000)
B.S. Lafayette College
Mathematics

Tyler Wood (2000)
B.A. University of Virginia, M.A. Georgetown University
English

Diana Yammin (1976)
B.A. Long Island University
Director of Studies

Catherine Jooyeon You (2006)
B.S. Tufts University, M.S. Northwestern University
Mathematics

BOARD OF TRUSTEES

ALUMNI COUNCIL

Richard B. Alexander '78

Andrew A. Bogle '90

Thomas M. Boyd '58

Noelle V.C. Brogi Grainger '89

Clyde R. Brown '49

Scott H. Buzby '47

Foster Devereux '56

Renée-Lauren V. Ellis '00

Hilary M. Fox '94

Robert H. Gregory '53

Elizabeth H. Guernsey '02

John C. Harvey '62

Peter Malin '69

Catherine E. Murphy East '92

Christopher Perry '87

Elijah D. Schachter '67

Boynton M. Schmitt '44

Peter S. Starbuck '69

Terrance H. Thoren '71

Elizabeth A. Uphoff Courtney '86

Roxalene E. Wadsworth '66

Theodore H. Wagenknecht '96

Jonathan D. Williams '74

PRIZE DAY SPEAKERS

1908
The Rev. Thomas H. Sill

1909
The Reverend James O. S. Huntington OHC

1910
Frederick Paul Keppel

1911
Frederick James Eugene Woodbridge

1912
Charles Sears Baldwin

1913
George W. Davison LL.D

1914
Randolph P. Titus '09

1915
Cuthbert Wright '10

1916
Douglas Crawford '10

1917
Edward T. Gushée '12

1918
The Rev. James O. S. Huntington OHC

1919
Chauncey Crawford '09
The Rev. S. C. Hughson

1920
The Rev. S. C. Hughson OHC

1921
The Hon. George Wharton Pepper

1922
The Rt. Rev. Charles B. Brewster
Fr. Huntington

1923
The Reverend James O.S. Huntington

1924
The Reverend James O.S. Huntington

1925
The Reverend James O.S. Huntington

1926
The Reverend James O.S. Huntington

1927
The Reverend James O.S. Huntington

1928
The Reverend James O.S. Huntington

1929
The Reverend James O.S. Huntington

1930
The Reverend James O.S. Huntington

1931
The Rt. Rev. Charles B. Colmore

1932
Bishop Ferry, Dr. Huntington
Fr. Hughson

1933
The Reverend James O.S. Huntington

1934
Father Hughson

1935
The Hon. John W. Davis

1936
Senator George Wharton Pepper

1937
The Hon. Wilbur Lucius Cross

1938
Father Alan Whittemore

1939
Father Alan Whittemore

1940
Senator Bennett Clark

1941
Father Alan Whittemore

1942
Colonel Fred W. Rankin

1943
Charles P. Harrington

1944
Edward Gushée '12

1945
Governor Raymond E. Baldwin

1946
Father John Butler OGS

1947
Father Robert Casey OGS

1948
Senator Raymond E. Baldwin

1949
The Rt. Rev. Jonathan Sherman '25

1950
The Very Rev. Lawrence Rose '18

1951
Vice Admiral Oscar Charles Badger

1952
The Rev. Paul Moore

1953
James Thorpe

1954
August Heckscher II

1955
The Rt. Rev. Henry Knox Sherrill

1956
The Rt. Rev. Stephen Bayne

195 7
Charles Collingwood

1958
Rear Admiral Chester C. Wood

1959
Sidney N. Towle '31

1960
Dr. Albert C. Jacobs

1961
The Reverend Albert Mollegen

1962
Cyrus R. Vance '35

1963
Dr. Reamer Kline

1964
Georges C. May

1965
Draper L. Kauffman '29

1967
Albert E. Holland

1968
Arjay R. Miller

1969
Dr. Anne Gary Pannell

1970
The Rt. Rev. Christoph Keller, Jr.

1971
Robert A. Ward '53

1972
Edmund Fuller

1973
Lowell P. Weicker

1974
Peter Bragdon

1975
Henry W. Bragdon '24

1976
Mary Wagley

1977
The Reverend Peter Woodward

1978
The Reverend John Verdery

1979
David Chipp

1980
Rowland Evans '39

1981
Dr. Elizabeth Morgan '63

1982
Edmund Fuller

1983
John F. Akers

1984
Serge A. Schmemann '63

1985
Galway Kinnell

1986
David E. Johnson '51

1987
Henry Kissinger

1988
David S. Ruder

1989
Congresswoman Nancy L. Johnson

1990
Nannerl Overholser Keohane

1991
William H. Armstrong Hon.'48

1992
Cornelia Keller Biddle '64

1993
Otis Benson Davis '42

1994
David C. Clapp '56

1995
Gwendolyn M. Parker '68

1996
Oscar De La Renta

1997
Donald Gowan '66

1998
The Hon. Alexandra Davis di Pentima '71

1999
Brandon Sweitzer '60

2000
The Rt. Rev. E. Don Taylor

2001
Laurance Rand

2002
Dr. Amy Williams

2003
Arthur Collins '48

2004
Joan M. Beattie

2005
Thomas K. Roney

2006
Sir Richard Dearlove

For additional information:

Kent School
Box 2006
Kent, Connecticut 06757

860-927-6000
www.kent-school.edu